MARCO ⊕ POLO

D1579933

TEN ERI FE

Azores (Port.)

ATLANTIC OCEAN

Madeira (Port.)

Canary Islands (Spain)

Western Sahara

Tenerife

FREE!

THE TOURING APP

shows you the way...
including routes and offline maps!

GET MORE OUT OF YOUR MARCO POLO GUIDE

IT'S AS SIMPLE AS THIS

1 go.marco-polo.com/ten

2 download and discover

GO!

WORKS OFFLINE!

SYMBOLS

INSIDER TIP	Insider Tip
★	Highlight
⬤⬤⬤⬤	Best of...
↘↙	Scenic view
♲	Responsible travel: for eco-logical or fair trade aspects
(*)	Telephone numbers that are not toll-free

PRICE CATEGORIES HOTELS

Expensive	over 150 euros
Moderate	80–150 euros
Budget	under 80 euros

Prices for a double room per night, with breakfast (in a hotel); without breakfast (in an apartments)

PRICE CATEGORIES RESTAURANTS

Expensive	over 25 euros
Moderate	15–25 euros
Budget	under 15 euros

Prices for a meal (typical for the restaurant) with starter and main course

CONTENTS

DID YOU KNOW?
Timeline → p. 14
Local specialities → p. 28
For bookworms and film buffs → p. 59
National holidays → p. 121
Budgeting → p. 125
Puerto Street Art → p. 126
Weather → p. 128
Currency converter → p. 129

MAPS IN THE GUIDEBOOK
(136 A1) Page numbers and coordinates refer to the road atlas
(0) Site/address located off the map
Coordinates are also given for places that are not marked on the road atlas

Map of Playa de las Américas/Los Cristianos on p. 86

(*□ A1*) refers to the removable pull-out map

INSIDE FRONT COVER:
The best Highlights

INSIDE BACK COVER:
Maps of Puerto de la Cruz and Santa Cruz de Tenerife

The best MARCO POLO Insider Tips

Our top 15 Insider Tips

INSIDER TIP **In the magic forest**

In the middle of the cloud-enveloped laurel forest, there's a little visitors' centre offering information on hiking in the Montañas de Anaga. Beneath it is a quaint path designed as an educational trail. You'll experience an "enchanted forest" in just an hour of walking → **p. 59**

INSIDER TIP **Music in the Auditorio**

Every week Tenerife's most extraordinary building is the venue for concerts in all musical genres → **p. 60**

INSIDER TIP **Organic finca**

Situated on the edge of a canyon, the Köllmann family runs the large organic Finca *El Quinto* with rustic houses in green surroundings, a paradise for nature lovers → **p. 51**

INSIDER TIP **The great outdoors**

Away from the coast Tenerife offers plenty of breathtaking encounters with nature. Dedicated active holidaymakers choose to stay in the *Luz del Mar* in Los Silos → **p. 38**

INSIDER TIP **Everything's fresh, everyone's happy!**

Vegetarian cuisine, tapas and good spirits in Bajamar: you'll feel right at home at *El León Cocina Natural!* → **p. 54**

INSIDER TIP **Troglodyte village**

At the point where the road ends below steep cliffs, a signposted footpath winds up to the tiny mountain village of *Chinamada*. The villagers still live in cave houses, just as they have for centuries → **p. 54**

INSIDER TIP **Beach for individualists**

A day away from the hustle and bustle? The perfect solution: the black sandy *Playa del Bollullo* with its beach bar near Puerto de la Cruz → **p. 48**

INSIDER TIP **Luxurious indulgence**

Intimate and exclusive residence with spacious suites and luxurious spa with a splendid view over the golf course to the mountains: the *Royal Garden Villas* offer peace and tranquillity → **p. 92**

INSIDER TIP Fish, fresh off the boat

San Andrés, a small coastal village, is a popular place for islanders (and few tourists) at weekends. The sea breeze must whet their appetite, because the restaurants do a roaring trade serving (usually) fresh fish and seafood → **p. 66**

INSIDER TIP Amuse-bouche

The dishes at the *Ardeola* restaurant in Garachico have a creative Canarian touch, are made with the freshest ingredients and are served in an exclusive atmosphere by an efficient, friendly staff → **p. 35**

INSIDER TIP The ultimate scenic route

A *panoramic road* extends the length of the Anaga Mountains with lookout points for fine views as far as the sea. It's the way to see the island's more primitive side (photo left) → **p. 101**

INSIDER TIP A close encounter with whales

Every day boats set sail from harbours in the southwest in search of dolphins and whales (photo below) → **p. 95**

INSIDER TIP When night falls

At the weekend, the place is abuzz: under an old stone bridge is *La Noria,* the centre of Santa Cruz's nightlife. Young revellers get together in the bars and bodegas in pedestrian zones with atmospheric lighting → **p. 64**

INSIDER TIP Mix with the locals

Get up with the chickens! Be a part of the community when you live at *Casa La Verita* or *Cha Carmen.* These traditional country hotels are nestled in the hills between Arico and Fasnia, well away from the tourist crowds → **p. 76**

INSIDER TIP Smooth sips at the wine house

The farmstead in El Sauzal attracts visitors with it's traditional architecture and a great view of the ocean. At the same time, you can really hit the bottle, Tenerife-style. *Casa del Vino,* the "wine house", offers the island's best wines for you to try at an affordable price → **p. 66**

BEST OF...

FOR FREE

● *A park above the town*

From the coastal vantage point in *Puerto de la Cruz* climb up past waterfalls and on to the *Parque Taoro* (photo). While the "Risco Bello" part of the park charges an admission fee, you can admire the wide plateau fringed by subtropical plants for free → p. 47

● *Natural swimming pools*

Ignore the waves crashing against the sea wall sending spray high into the air, while you swim serenely in the *natural pools of Bajamar*. Few other places in the north offer the same safe bathing opportunities → p. 53

● *From fruit market to art showroom*

The *Centro de Arte La Recova* used to be a busy fruit market hall in Santa Cruz, but now it is used to display art – photographs, avantgarde and the out-of-the-ordinary → p. 66

● *Visitor centre with botanical garden*

In the *Centro de Visitantes El Portillo* you can be part of the island's geological history. The volcanic tunnel quakes, red-hot lava flows and the room rumbles. Round off your visit with a tour of the botanical rock garden replete with native alpine flora → p. 71

● *Daydreaming at the sea*

Against the backdrop of five-star hotels that you have to dig deep into your pockets for, you'll find the small but lovely beach of *Bahía del Duque* – where everyone can put down a towel for free! Breakwaters protect against the surf, and the white sands are as soft as velvet... → p. 90

● *Art and meditation*

Cristino de Vera uses lots of little dots to create paintings that will transfix you in silence and beauty. The collection of 100 paintings can be viewed for free in the beautiful manor house of La Laguna. Worthwhile even for those who aren't into art! → p. 56

◖◗◖◗◖◗●◖◗ Dots in guidebook refer to "Best of..." tips

● *A dragon tree with no dragons*
It has become one of Tenerife's trademarks. Although the tree with its lush crown is actually a type of lily, it can live for up to 1,000 years. The largest and most beautiful *drago* grows in Icod de los Vinos → p. 38

● *Eat like the Guanches*
It's a cereal, roasted and finely ground – *gofio*, the nutrient-rich staple food of the Guanches. Frowned upon for a long time as poor man's food, it is now a popular ingredient in the new Canarian cuisine, e.g. in El Duende → pp. 26, 48

● *Gaze into space*
Stand on the roof of the island and pretend you're an actor in a science-fiction film – the metallic white towers of the *Observatorio del Teide* (photo) look straight up into the clear blue sky which offers fine glimpses into space → p. 71

● *The pine tree – a survivor*
In the forest belt below the Cañadas grows the Canarian pine. With its extremely long needles it "combs" moisture from the clouds, while the thick bark even protects it from fire. One outstanding example is the *Pino Gordo* → p. 77

● *Sun-ripened*
Many of the exotic fruits that can grow in the "eternal spring" are made into jams, chutneys and compotes. For the best selection visit *Delicias del Sol* in Chío – everything here is organic → p. 95

● *Stone pyramids*
In many places stones are carefully laid to create rural and urban walls. But in Güímar they were made into mysterious pyramids. They suggest that even before Christopher Columbus the Canary Islands were a staging post between the Old and the New World → p. 75

● *Filigree rosettes*
The women of Vilaflor have made a virtue out of necessity. To supplement the family budget, in the evening they get together and make lace rosettes. In this mountain village bed covers, table lace and shawls are still made using the traditional method → p. 77

ONLY ON

BEST OF...

● *In the cave of the wind*
High above Icod de los Vinos is one of the world's longest lava tunnels. A short section of it is open to the public. But first of all do check out the *Cueva del Viento* Visitor Centre, which explains how the tunnel came into being → **p. 40**

● *Lost in space*
The most interesting museum in La Laguna is the *Museo de la Ciencia*, which aims to unravel some of the mysteries of the cosmos. The Milky Way, supernovae, black holes – all are clearly explained → **p. 55**

● *Island history and island stories*
At the *Museo de la Naturaleza y el Hombre*, you can spend (at least) half a rainy day looking around and delving into the island's history. You'll learn how Tenerife formed, how it was populated and everything about its first inhabitants → **p. 61**

● *In the shopping mall*
Stroll, browse and shop on seven floors for the latest fashions sorted by brand, cosmetics, perfume and jewellery. The food and drink section at *El Corte Inglés* is also impressive → **p. 63**

● *A pyramid with life inside*
Colonnades, temples and right in the middle the *Pirámide de Arona* – modelled on classical antiquity in downtown Playa de las Américas. There's a show every night in the pyramid. No gladiators, instead a troupe of flamenco dancers fired up by passion → **p. 89**

● *The bustle of the market hall*
At the weekend everyone makes a pilgrimage to the market (the one in *Adeje* is always lively). Fresh produce supplied by local farmers at affordable prices. Round off the morning with a glass of wine and a tapa in the market bar → **p. 90**

RAIN

RELAX AND CHILL OUT
Take it easy and spoil yourself

● *Enjoy a sundowner in style*
If you love to watch the sun set, then the beach bar at the *Villa Cortés* is the place to go. Order a beer, let your mind wander and watch the windsurfers ride the last waves of the day → **p. 87**

● *A white aquatic landscape*
Lago de Martíanez in Puerto de la Cruz is a vast pool area designed with many curving contours (photo). Palm trees provide shade and palisade fences keep the city clamour away → **p. 116**

● *Refuel in the Hotel Mencey*
After a stroll in the capital, Santa Cruz, you can regain your strength in the *Mencey*. This grand hotel in the old style has a club bar, a garden café and the restaurant is undoubtedly one of the best on the island → **p. 64**

● *Take the red bus*
Get comfy on the double-decker in *Santa Cruz* and let the city roll past. You can put in your headphones to listen to interesting facts about the sights along the route. You can get off and back on again at any time at 13 different stations → **p. 65**

● *Relax in Oriental style*
The island's newest spa is also the smartest one – it's in the south and occupies a majestic location overlooking a beautiful beach. As the name *Thai Zen SPAce* suggests, the treatments follow Oriental relaxation techniques → **p. 89**

● *Los roques de Garcia*
If you get up early or leave it until later on in the afternoon, you will have one of the grandest landscapes in the Canaries at the *Mirador de Los Roques* pretty well all to yourself → **p. 70**

● *In the shadow of exotic plants*
IIn the *Jardin Botánico* in Puerto de la Cruz, tropical plants form a primeval jungle. Sit by the pond or the fountain and let body and soul unwind → **p. 46**

DISCOVER TENERIFE!

No, it's not lost any of its fascination. Planes circle it at respectful distance, before heading in to land on Tenerife. Visible from many miles, it shows the way. It's become a symbol for the island. Often dense cloud cover separates it from the world below. The Pico del Teide is the *king of all volcanoes*, surveying from his great height the hostile lunar landscape below. For us it's still an impressive sight, but for our forebears it was greatly feared. There was an eruption on its northern slopes as recently as 1909.

Legends in Antiquity already told of an island called *Nivaria* or the "snowy one". Passing mariners couldn't fail to see the white tip, but they did not discover the island itself. The Guanches, Tenerife's first settlers, feared that an angry god, Guayote, was orchestrating Teide's eruptions. Columbus saw the sparks and smoke it spat out as a bad omen for his first voyage of discovery. In 1799 Alexander von Humboldt, who ascended the mountain, was struck by the fact that at daybreak the first rays of sunshine illuminated the summit, while on the coast darkness still reigned. The Canarian day begins and ends on Mount Teide, at 3,718m (12,198ft) *Spain's highest mountain.* Despite the southern location of the Canary Islands, it often wears a snow cap in winter.

The north coast of the island is often wild, steep and rugged, as here near Las Aguas

Tenerife, with 2,034 km² (785 sq miles) the largest of the seven Islands of Eternal Spring, as the Canaries were known in the era of Homer, inspires through its contrasts: a blue ocean, great beaches, rugged cliffs, deep gorges, dense forests, barren wastes and Mount Teide volcano rising out of a bizarre sea of lava – an opulent display of nature's diversity. Wander through colonial towns, explore museums and churches – culturally Tenerife has a lot to offer, too. Sit with the locals in down-to-earth bars, enjoy their traditional food, drink their strong wines and share in their lively festivals. Surf, dive, hike, cycle, turn night into day or simply lie back and relax – there is no place for boredom on Tenerife. And the sun will keep shining – throughout the whole year.

Since 1100 BC
During their voyages of discovery the Phoenicians and later the Carthaginians arrive on the Canary Islands. First mention by Homer and Hesiod

5th century BC
Probably the first settlement on the archipelago by Berber tribes from North Africa

1496
The Spaniard Alonso Fernández de Lugo conquers Tenerife, the last of all the islands in the archipelago, and founds the settlement now called La Laguna

1701
Monks establish the first university on the Canary Islands in La Laguna

But many people get a shock when they arrive at Reina Sofía airport: barren urban sprawl as far as the eye can see, the south is bleak and parched. It quickly becomes apparent that water is a rare and precious commodity here. Once great forests extended across Tenerife, streams trickled down from the mountains. But at the end of the 15th century the Spanish colonists set about exploiting both man and

Water is a rare and precious commodity

nature. First they subjugated the Guanches and then they felled the laurel and pine trees, on whose long needles the moisture from the clouds clung, before it dripped to the ground. Erosion followed, *Tenerife's ecosystem* had been badly damaged. Today, pine forests are only found in the interior, the laurel survives in the Anaga Mountains in the northeast.

The Guanches, and later the Europeans, preferred to settle in the cool upland plateau of La Laguna and in the Valle de la Orotava, *Tenerife's green lung*. They get the benefit of the northeast trade winds. Moist winds blow constantly against the north coast of Tenerife at altitudes of between 700–1,700m, but the central highlands block their passage. The clouds that form deposit rainfall and provide shade, which in turn lowers the temperature and helps to supply the vegetation with water. It's always cooler in these parts than in the south of the island. However, there is no need to fear the torrid heat of Africa – the continent is only some 300 km (180 miles) away. The climate here is surprisingly benign. It is indeed like an *eternal spring*, which means mild temperatures – barely over 30° C in summer, rarely below 20° C in winter. Warm trade winds and the cool Canarian current in the Atlantic help to maintain a steady balance. Several times a year, however, the island experiences the *calima,* a hot, dusty desert wind that blows directly across from the Sahara. It often hangs over the archipelago for several days. The air never seems to move and breathing can be difficult. When the wind moves away, a fine layer of desert sand remains on buildings and on plants.

The holiday destinations of Los Cristianos and Playa de las Américas in the south have simply everything today's tourists could wish for. In just 50 years, an otherwise barren region has been transformed by beach resorts with apartment complexes, hotels and amusement parks – albeit for the price of living in a *tourist ghetto*. A hundred

1706
The volcanic eruption of Montaña Negra destroys large parts of the port of Garachico, but in the process new land forms in the northwest of Tenerife, now called Isla Baja

1797
Admiral Horatio Nelson invades Santa Cruz, but is repelled

1852
Queen Isabel II grants the Canary Islands the status of a free trade zone, British influence grows thereafter

End of 19th Century
The cultivation and export of bananas brings economic prosperity to Tenerife

years ago, however, Puerto de la Cruz in the north was a retreat for well-heeled English visitors escaping miserable winters back home. Many took lodgings in the former port of La Orotava. Locals and visitors found the arrangement to be of mutual benefit. The tourists enjoyed a well-established urban setting and the Canary islanders were perfectly happy to do business with them.

Nowadays, the aim is to move away from tourism monoculture. So there's energetic support for solutions that point in other, promising directions. This, of course, would hardly have been possible without the plentiful flow of EU funding. It's found its way into vineyards and honey production, fish processing and livestock, and arts and crafts and the textile industry – and the results speak for themselves. The island's cheese regularly scoops up international awards, the wine is of considerably high quality and the honey, e.g. from the blossoms of the native *tajinaste*, has an exotic taste. These products are already sold throughout the archipelago and in delicatessens all around the world; they're available everywhere through the *island's own online shop* (www.tucanarias.com).

> **Cheese, wine and honey from Tenerife are of considerably high quality.**

But if you really want to get to know the country and the people, you need to explore the *zona Metropolitana*. This is the name used to refer to the old and new capital (La Laguna/Santa Cruz) collectively. Almost one third of the 800,000 *Tinerfeños* live in this agglomeration. A lot has happened here in recent years. The historic centre of La Laguna has been freed from traffic and completely restored and it now enjoys *Unesco*

1927
Tenerife, La Palma, La Gomera and Hierro combine to create the Province of Santa Cruz de Tenerife

1936
General Franco stages a military coup on Tenerife and forms a bridgehead for an assault on the government in Madrid

1960 onwards
The island enjoys steady growth with the advent of cheap air travel and package holidays

1986
Spain becomes a member of the European Union

2009–15
A consequence of the global financial crisis: ongoing high levels of unemployment despite growing tourist flows.

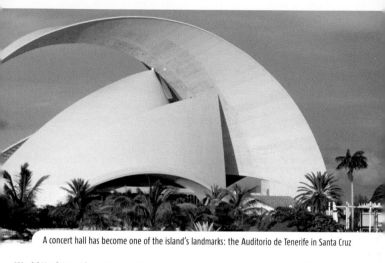

A concert hall has become one of the island's landmarks: the Auditorio de Tenerife in Santa Cruz

World Heritage Site status. In Santa Cruz, internationally renowned architects designed emblematic buildings, such as the Auditorium, the Congress Hall and the TEA Arts Centre. There were many ambitious plans for the future, e.g. a facelift for the sea front as far as the beach in San Andrés 10 km (6 miles) away. But as a result of the global financial crisis all these grandiose plans have had to be shelved. Though the Canaries have been "war profiteers" for years, since many holidaymakers that used to travel to North Africa or the Middle East now opt for the archipelago, the stampede of tourists has still hardly managed to decrease the unemployment rate (25 per cent in 2016). Hotel owners aren't

> **In the countryside there's a world that harks back to a different era**

hiring anyone new, instead getting their existing staff to take care of the increased workload. But visitors will hardly notice the impact on everyday life. Despite the adverse circumstances, the Canary islanders stay cheerful. The general view is: "We can't change anything, so what's the point of complaining?" And so the Canary islanders keep celebrating at *fiestas*, call in at the café or their favourite bar, take a late evening stroll through the parks and stop everything for a siesta between 1pm and 5pm.

If you explore the countryside, however, you will be surprised to find a world that harks back to a different era: farmers loading up their donkeys, old men passing the time at the plaza, women dressed in black labouring in the fields, huts whose roofs sag from the burden of the decades. A rather *Spartan lifestyle* continues very much as it did 60 years ago all over Tenerife. At the beginning of the 20th century, thousands of *Tinerfeños* emigrated to South America and to Cuba to escape famine at home. Today, the Canary islanders are as one with the entire Spanish nation – the crises of the present day can be overcome at home.

WHAT'S HOT

1 Be energy aware

Go green ⚛ The five-day film festival *Festival Internacional de Cine Medioambiental de Canarias (www.ficmec.es)* is held in early summer in Garachico showing films on environmental issues – and with open-air screenings in the courtyard of the Franciscan monastery. Throughout the year, the *Instituto Tecnologico y de Energias Renovables (Granadilla de Abona, www.iter.es) (photo)* keeps consumers informed about the latest developments in green energy. There is even an educational trail, which illustrates the benefits of alternatives, such as photovoltaic solar panels, wind and geothermal energy. The island's trams, incidentally, are powered by solar energy through PV panels *(metrotenerife.com)*.

2

Gays welcome

Places to be There's always fierce competition between Tenerife and Gran Canaria. So it was inevitable that Tenerife wanted to challenge its sister island's status as an LGBT paradise. The most important beach haunt of local and visiting gays is already the natural *Playa de la Tejita* to the north of El Médano, also popular with nudists. After sunset, gays flutter into the *Butterfly Club (C.C. Salytien / Av. Rafael Puig Lluvina 10)* in Playa de las Américas.

3 La Laguna

New life La Laguna is back on the map again, especially in the former capital's tapas bars and bodegas *(www.aytolalaguna.com)*. It's now a fashionable spot for young islanders and there's a real buzz in the Old Town in the evening. The bars Tasca El Tonique (C/ Heraclio Sánchez 23) and Tasca 61 (C/ Viana 61) are popular meeting places, as is Bodegón Viana (Viana 35).

World Cheese Award

World-class cheese There's not a single international competition that Tenerife's dairy products come away from empty-handed. *Granja Los Palmeros/Queso Montesdeoca (Subida a Tijoco Alto)* near Guía de Isora, supplied with the milk of 1000 goats, is almost always represented. Three generations of cheese makers ensure top quality. Nearby, *El Guanche (Ctra. Guía de Isora-Chío 13)* specialises in smoked cheese. *Flor de Güimar (Ctra. Güimar-Arafo)* also focuses on this delicacy, using "cold smoke" from tree heath to add a hint of spice. Queso5senti2 primarily produces flower cheese: juice from the thistle flower solidifies the milk and gives it a tart flavour. Try it out at La Laguna's groceries!

Back to the roots

Lo nuestro A stylised canary on regional foods will wink at you, and you'll be met everywhere by palm and sea logos. Switch on Canary Islands television on Saturday night at 7pm and watch the popular folklore show *Tenderete*. Young men and women in traditional garb sing about love, saying goodbye and leaving the islands, although now-adays, hardly any Canary Islanders emigrate overseas. Those who inherit little homes in the country spruce them up and live in them just like their ancestors did – if possible, with a cage full of warbling birds, a *pila*, a stone water filter and an *estanque*, a water tank. Add in a glass of wine from the home bodega and a weekend barbecue – and you've got yourself the new old Canary Islands feeling. *Lo nuestro* (Ours, i.e. Canarian) is considered a seal of quality!

IN A NUTSHELL

DON'T GET HURT!

Lucha canaria, Canarian wrestling, dates from the time of the Guanches. Twelve contestants in two teams compete in pairs against each other in a sand-lined ring about 15 m (50 ft) in diameter. In a clearly defined starting position they lean forward face-to-face and attempt to grab the rolled-up trouser leg of the opponent with their left hand. During the match, which lasts a maximum of three minutes, the *luchadores* must try, using different grips, to throw their opponent to the ground. If you floor your opponent twice, you win. The team with the most victories wins the contest. If you would like to watch a match, enquire at the tourist information office about

fixtures; every major town has its own arena *(terrero de lucha canaria)*.

DRAGONS & VIPERS

No plant has captured the imagination of the Canary islanders quite so much as the dragon tree. This relative of the yucca, became extinct beyond the Macaronesian islands (Canaries, Madeira, Azores, Cape Verde) 20 million years ago, although close relatives do exist in Africa and Asia. The Guanches regarded the tree as sacred, largely because of its resin, known as "dragon's blood", which turns dark red when exposed to the air and in the distant past was used in the preparation of medicinal potions and ointments. If you cut a

Of Guanches and dragon trees – Tenerife has much more to offer than just sunshine, beaches and the Pico del Teide

branch from the *drago*, it grows back as quickly as "the head of a dragon'". That is why the early naturalists gave the tree its fairytale-inspired botanical name *Dracaena drago*. And the locals still revere their dragon trees. There's hardly a garden in the Canary Islands that would do without one.

Another fantastic plant is the viper's bugloss, or more specifically, the Tenerife bugloss (Echium wildpretii). Its botanical name refers to the Swiss botanist Hermann Wildpret, but it's a true

Tinerfeño. It has a 2 m (6 ft) high inflorescence that rises upward like a viper enchanted by a snake charmer and is studded with thousands of small, glowing red blossoms – no bee (or person) can miss it during its flowering stage from May to June! The viper's bugloss is robust and grows well above the timberline – a burning exclamation mark amidst an Alpine lava landscape. Close relatives of the Tenerife bugloss grow at lower elevations, but they are smaller and their blossoms are blue or white.

ISLAND OF THE ARTS

In earlier times, if you lived on the Canaries and wanted to become an artist, you had to get away from the seclusion of the islands as quickly as possible. But one *Tinerfeño* artist did succeed in bringing back to the Atlantic island much of what he had experienced and learned while living in Paris among Picasso's contemporaries. In 1935 Óscar Domínguez, and none other than André Breton, organised a major Surrealism exhibition in Tenerife's capital, thus bringing to this distant Atlantic province avant-garde art from all over the world. His artistic awakening was brought to an abrupt end by the Spanish Civil War (1936–39). However, the basis for later artistic activities had been created.

Today there is not only a permanent exhibition of Domínguez's works in the prestigious *Tenerife Espacio de Las Artes (TEA)*, but also in several other renowned galleries, e.g. the *Galería Leyendecker (Rambla 86 | www.leyendecker.net)*, and the *El Tanque* cultural centre *(Calle 70)* in Santa Cruz, and the *Fundación Cristino de Vera* and the *Sala Conca* in La Laguna. The works of many modern artists are also often shown in temporary exhibitions at the *MACEW (Casa de Aduana | Calle Las Lonjas s/n)* in Puerto de la Cruz's former customs house above the tourist information office.

The multi-day *MUECA* street festival *(www.festivalmueca.com)* devoted to art in many of its forms brings colour to the streets of Puerto de la Cruz. The most important art event staged on Tenerife

Dragon trees such as this magnificent specimen in Los Realejos can grow to a height of 20 m/66 ft

today is the *Foto-Noviembre* photography festival *(www.fotonoviembre.com)*, where recent projects from all over the world are on display.

IT CAN'T GET ANY BRIGHTER

No one thinks of Tenerife when, every year, footage of the colourful Brazilian carnivals appears on television. But the exuberant spectacle on this Canary Island easily bears comparison with Rio's samba party. Months of preparatory work are needed for the wild weeks in February and March. *Carrozas* or floats have to be built and decorated, costumes must be sewn, masks and disguises carefully crafted. *Murgas*, groups dressed in colourful jester-like costumes, compete with one another to make the best outfits, to sing the cheekiest songs and to play the weirdest music. During the *desfiles*, the processions, they dance and frolic noisily through the streets. In Santa Cruz de Tenerife there are often tens of thousands of revellers on the move, forming a heaving sea of bodies.

Each night after these parades, which are transmitted live on national Spanish television, is a *mogollón*: *Tinerfeños* dance to Latin rhythms until the early hours of the morning. And it goes on for days, and weeks.

The official climax is the election of the *Reina del Carnaval*. It is not beauty that determines who is crowned as carnival queen, but the grace with which she manages to carry the extravagant costume – itself worth as much as a midrange car and weighing only a little less.

The grand finale for the *carnaval* is the *Entierro de la Sardina*, the burial of the sardine. Once again there is a spectacular, colourful parade, but this time a huge cardboard sardine is dragged through the streets. It ends with a pyrotechnic explosion of Roman candles, rockets and firecrackers. Holidaymakers are encouraged to take part in all events. Ask at the tourist information offices for details.

MADONNA OF THE SEA

Lots of fuss for a little figure: A town is named after her, huge events are organised for her, taxi drivers drive with her image and calendars bear her likeness. The *Virgin de Candelaria* is the crowned queen of Tenerife, and has been the island's patron saint for over 500 years. Her career began in the early 15th century when a few Guanches found a Gothic statue of the Madonna and Child, which had been washed ashore near Candelaria. Legend has it that the fearful shepherds wanted to throw stones at it, but their arms became paralysed as they started to throw. Impressed by the figure's obvious magical powers, the aboriginal Canarians transported the figure into a cave and began to worship it.

Later on, when Catholic missionaries arrived on the island, it was easy for them to use this belief to convert the Guanches to the faith of that "magical woman". The statue was given the name Our Lady of Candelaria and a small church was built there in her honour. However in 1826, a freak wave washed the church and the Madonna out to sea. The present statue was made in 1827 by a local artist. The Virgin's complexion, as well as that of the child, is almost as black as the volcanic sand on the beach. And of course, a new church was built soon after.

MYSTERIOUS GUANCHES

Little is known about the island's original inhabitants, whose name translates as "sons of Tenerife". They colonised the archipelago from the 3rd century BC, arriving in several waves, and it is thought they are descended from the light-skinned Berbers of North Africa. The Guanches were primarily farmers who reared goats and sheep. They were Cruz and also in the mysterious Pirámides de Güímar.

SHADY HOUSES

You may be surprised to see that many elaborately crafted wooden doors and

Snow on the sunny island: take the cable to the winter wonderland of Teide National Park

ruled by a type of king, called a *mencey*. When the Spanish settlers arrived on the Canaries, the nine sons of the mencey Bezenuria ruled. Larger-than-life bronze statues of them line the waterfront promenade of Plaza Patrona de Canarias in Candelaria. The Guanches lived mostly in caves, where they buried their artfully mummified dead.

The Europeans subjugated, enslaved or killed the natives. However, the survivors were quickly integrated into the population of the conquerors. Their legacy can be seen in the *Museo del Hombre y la Naturaleza* in Santa Cruz, in the *Museo Arqueológico* in Puerto de la

windows are locked and shuttered up – and that not a soul can be seen on the fantastically carved balconies. But where the sun beats down all year round, people are more drawn to shady retreats than to the open air. Closely latticed shutters allow the air to circulate, but they also block the sun, creating an air-conditioning effect.

The *façades* are white as chalk – to reflect the sunlight. Bare house corners, door and window frames cut from blocks of rough volcanic stone and pale red roof tiles reveal strong contrasts. The hub of a house is the *patio*, the inner courtyard, which provides access to all the rooms through arcades on each floor. There will often be luxurious plant-ings, and there might even be a fountain, to create a cool, green retreat from the warm Canarian climate.

Churches and town houses have carved and finely painted timber ceilings inside, often in Moorish-inspired Mudéjar style. La Orotava and La Laguna showcase lovely examples of Canarian architecture. The best preserved mountain village in Tenerife is Masca, where the houses are dry stone walled, – that is, they use no mortar.

SNOW IN ETERNAL SPRING

It's only 300 km (180 miles) to the Sahara Desert – so can it really snow here? It can, and it does. Teide National Park lies at an elevation of over 2,000 m (6,560 ft) and there, temperatures can dip below freezing. When it does snow, warmly-wrapped Canary Islanders will make the trek to the top in order to enjoy the white stuff.

The snow and ice played an important commercial role on Tenerife at the time of the Spanish conquest. A new occupation, the ice vendors or *neveros*, emerged. They earned a living from first making the dangerous multiple-day ascent on foot to the top of Teide, then transporting the cold cargo, either on beasts of burden or on their backs, down into the villages and selling it.

SOS H$_2$O

There has to be a downside if the sun always shines: a shortage of water. In earlier times, there were many rivers on Tenerife and the dense pine and laurel forests absorbed the moisture from the trade winds. Wells and shafts stretching for kilometres, known as galleries, were driven deep into the mountains, reaching underground water supplies, and this kept the farmers' crops irrigated.

But since then, most of the trees have been felled and many of the wells have run dry. Rainwater is collected in a few reservoirs. But it is mainly seawater desalination plants that supply the holiday resorts of Tenerife; there are also nine golf courses that need a lot of water.

Water obtained in this way requires money and energy, the latter is being generated mainly through the environmentally harmful burning of oil. Newer plants are being converted to the more environmentally friendly reverse osmosis procedure, whereby the salt is mechanically removed from the seawater. It is forced through a semi-permeable membrane, which lets through the water molecules, but blocks the larger salt particles. Although tourism uses only about 10 per cent of the water – agriculture takes the lion's share, about 70 per cent – please set a good example: don't waste water.

WHO'S THAT CHIRPING?

Its plumage is yellow, its song melodic. It usually sits in a cage and warbles to the delight of its owner. Even in the remotest corners of the world, it is just as much at home in a hut as in a palace. Many people are familiar with the canary, but they may not know that it is also the name of an archipelago in the Atlantic. The canary is a relative of the wild *Serenus canaria*, a bird which still inhabits the archipelago's forests. It also sings beautifully, but its appearance is not so spectacular. This is why it was modified through selective breeding, until it acquired its present form.

FOOD & DRINK

For millennia, the Canary Islands' staple has been *gofio*, a flour made of roasted maize, millet or barley. It was easy to farm this grain, and even possible to do so in the mountains on terraced fields.

Wherever water gushed through the gorges, millstones ground flour. This yellow or light brown powder is a filling, protein-rich food and best of all, it is always available and very versatile. In addition, it is flavour-neutral, so it mixes well with other ingredients. The Guanches conjured up bread and soups from *gofio*. If you see *gofio escaldado*, a *caldo* (broth) made with thickened gofio flour, then do give it a try. True to the original style, it's spooned up with raw red onion slices. Now innovative chefs even mix finely ground ● *gofio* with ice cream and

banana purée – for daring, but still very tasty creations.

Soups and stews are very popular. Freshly-prepared *sopas* are served at almost every restaurant that specialises in local cuisine. One worthy of recommendation is the *potaje canario*, a hearty vegetable soup. A somewhat spicy soup is *potaje de berros*. Its most important ingredient is large bitter-cress and it is readily served in a wooden bowl. For *Tinerfeños* survival depended on the optimum use of the available resources. They tended **sheep and goats** and later on began to hunt rabbits. But meat and fish remained a luxury that, until the 20th century, few islanders could afford. Before the era of refrigeration, to protect against spoi-

Gofio, mojo and bienmesabe: international fast food is passé – discover the advantages of traditional cuisine!

lage, animal produce had to be stored in brine or dried. So the islanders developed a speciality known as *adobos*. Food was marinated for weeks, sometimes months, in **hot sauces** made from oil, vinegar, bay leaf, herbs, garlic and pepper; only then did its typical flavour develop. There were no leftovers at the preparation stage. Everything went into the pot and dishes with curious names such as *ropa vieja* emerged – in English it means "old clothes", referring with delightful clarity to the recycled ingre-

dients it contained. *Ropa vieja, puchero* and *rancho canario*, **meat and vegetable stews**, are now, of course, freshly prepared with pork, chick peas, potatoes, pasta, onions, saffron, garlic and spicy *chorizo* sausage. These are among the tastiest – and most traditional – dishes Tenerife's cuisine has to offer. So over the generations, Canarian cuisine developed its own character.

The traditional accompaniment are *papas arrugadas*, now a snack much-loved by tourists. The famous "wrinkly

LOCAL SPECIALITIES

baifito en adobo – marinated kid is eaten with salad and *papa*

bienmesabe – translates as "it tastes good to me" – a sticky, golden-brown dessert made with honey, almonds, egg yolks and lemon (photo right)

caldo de pescado – a thin fish soup with potatoes and herbs

carajacas – calves', pigs' or chicken liver chopped into pieces and pickled

cherne al cilantro – pan-fried Canarian gilthead bream in coriander sauce

conejo en salmorejo – rabbit in a marinade of bay leaves, garlic and wine

gofio escaldado – *gofio*, thickened with a broth of *caldo de pescado* into a creamy, maize-yellow porridge, with herbs and paprika to taste

mojo rojo – velvety to runny hot sauce of red chillies, oil, garlic, vinegar and salt. Accompanies meat dishes and *papas arrugadas*

mojo verde – like *mojo rojo*, but green instead of red chillies and lots of parsley. Served with fish and *papas arrugadas*

papas arrugadas – Canarian potatoes boiled in brine, always eaten with its wrinkly (in Spanish: *arrugado*) skin (photo left)

pella – bread-like dough made from *gofio*, water and salt. Eaten sliced with *sancocho canario*

potaje canario – thick soup of chickpeas, potatoes, seasonal vegetables and maize

potaje de berros – mild watercress stew with bacon, potatoes, pumpkin, maize, yams. Gofio is then stirred in

rancho canario – stew of chickpeas, potatoes, pork, noodles, onions, garlic, *chorizo*

ropa vieja – thick stew of chickpeas, meat, vegetables and potatoes

sancocho canario – salted fish, boiled and then eaten with vegetables, *mojo* and *pella*

potatoes" are served in every restaurant. They are a special variety: small, dark on the outside, yellow inside. Accompanying the potatoes is another delicacy that many will be familiar with, **mojo**. This spicy sauce – it could be red or green – comes with practically every dish.

Fish and seafood now dominate Tenerife's menus. Historically, that's illogical, given that the Guanches were rather poor fishermen. Nowadays cooking methods mainly reflect the ways of Spanish immigrants. *Vieja, cherne, sama, caballa, bocinegro* taste *best a la plancha*, which means fried with a little oil on a hot metal plate. These are all rather firm Canarian fish, which reveal their full flavour when served with a salad and *mojo*. Also very much in demand are *pulpo* and *choco*, two types of squid.

Cocina casera, today's typical Canarian fare, consists of an eclectic mix of dishes from all over the world: fennel from Andalusia, yams from Africa, saffron from La Mancha, stodgy desserts from England, pasta from Italy and chayote from Venezuela. These dishes are a reminder of the fact that for 400 years the Canary Islands were at the hub of three continents. To round off a good meal without a dessert would be a criminal offence. In addition to practically every kind of fruit – bananas, oranges and apricots to papayas, guavas and mangoes, all of which are harvested on the island – comes *flan*, a caramel custard and now a very popular dessert. However, the highlight of any Canarian dessert menu has to be *bienmesabe*, a blend of honey, lime or lemon, almonds and eggs. Every meal has to be rounded off with a *cortado* or a *solo* – an espresso with or without milk.

With their meal, the locals will drink Tenerife's slightly bitter keg beer, **Dorada**, or a bottle of the **island's wine**. Among all the islands in the archipelago, Tenerife is the main wine producer and, in fact, has a long tradition with the fruit of the vine. Cultivation started shortly after the Conquest, and before long many barrels were finding their way to the European mainland. But the colonial rivalry between Spain and England destroyed what was a thriving trade. Phylloxera infestation caused further damage to the island's wine industry. The tide turned only after Spain joined the EU; money from Brussels was invested in agriculture and the *Tinerfeños* began to rediscover their vine-growing expertise. Family wineries were modernised, new bodegas were opened and

White or red – Tenerife's vintages are much sought after

before long wines from Tenerife were winning international prizes. Today on Tenerife there are five different *Denominaciones de Origen* (Protected Designation of Origin) corresponding to the regions different in climate and geology. Grapes are harvested in September, so that the young wine can start to flow at Martinmas in early November – the wine festivals then take place in Icod de los Vinos, Puerto de la Cruz and Tacoronte. The best place to taste the island's vintages is the ● *Casa del Vino* (p. 66) in El Sauzal, just north of Puerto de la Cruz. For a small outlay, you can sample several different varieties.

SHOPPING

When it comes to shopping, the locals invariably choose Santa Cruz, because it boasts a well-stocked department store, namely El Corte Inglés, as well as many smart boutiques. For food and drink, the farmers' markets *(mercadillos de agricultor)* are the automatic choice. These are held at weekends, notably, for example, in Tacoronte.

For traditional handicrafts, of which you will find a wide choice on Tenerife, La Orotava is by far the best place – a walk through the Old Town is like a journey back in time. Beautifully carved balconies and arcades attest to the superior craftsmanship of Canarian woodcarvers. And even behind the facades the old traditions are maintained. La Orotava is the centre of Tenerife's artesanía, the island's handicrafts. Original crafts come supplied with a guarantee and the manufacturer's name when you buy in the shops belonging to the state Artenerife chain, which also ensures that the artisans are fairly rewarded. They are to be found in Santa Cruz, Puerto de la Cruz, La Orotava, Playa de las Américas and Los Cristianos. *www.artenerife.com*

EMBROIDERY

Canarian embroidery, particularly the open threadwork style, has a long tradition on Tenerife; it is of outstanding quality, but the real thing comes at a price. With this type of sewing, material, stretched tightly on a wooden frame, is partially unravelled and then, using a complicated hemstitching technique *(calado)*, patterns or motifs, such as suns or roses, stitched on. The finished items are sold as tablecloths, table mats and handkerchiefs.

FLOWERS

One delightful souvenir is the exotic bird of paradise plant *(strelitzia)*, which is cultivated on Tenerife. You can even buy it at the airport shop after check-in. As an alternative, you can purchase a bag of drago seeds and cultivate *dragon* trees!

FOOD & DRINK

The best souvenir for friends and family back home is nearly always something to eat or drink. And here the Canary Islands can offer a great selection – cheese from happy goats, the delicious *bienmesabe* dessert, liqueurs made from palm juice or bananas and locally-made cakes and pastries. *Gofio*, the flour of the native Guanches, can be bought in many super-

Outlet centres, luxury boutiques, farmers' markets – shopping is a tonne of fun for the *Tinerfeños*, so the range of products has to be big

markets. Or it can be bought directly from the miller at one of Tenerife's last working flour mills in La Orotava. You will need to find *C/ Doctor Domingo González García 3 (Mon–Fri 8am–1pm and 3pm–7pm, Sat 8am–1pm)*. Teobaldo Méndez has won many awards for his delicious treats. In his shop, *El Aderno (daily 9am–8:30pm | La Alhóndiga 8 | www.eladerno.com)* in Buenavista del Norte, the best *pâtissier* on Tenerife sells traditional Canarian pastries, such as *rosquetes, truchas* and *merengues.* Teobaldo's secret is no surprise: he uses only the best ingredients.

Tenerife's wines are among the best in the Canaries. Grape varieties, such as *listán blanco, listán negra* and *negramoll*, which produce light, dry wines, are grown at altitudes of up to 1,600 m (5,250 ft), mainly in the northwest. "Frontos", a white wine produced from organically grown grapes in the Abona region, is currently enjoying plaudits from wine connoisseurs. Other wines from the island are available in bodegas, wine stores and good supermarkets.

POTTERY

Alfarería – bowls, plates, jugs and drinking vessels – were essential commodities for everyday life and would be produced with no particular artistic ambitions. Today it is their sheer simplicity that gives them their special appeal. In the village of Arguayo near Santiago del Teide, the pottery is still made using traditional methods. Without a potter's wheel, thick rolls of clay are stacked on top of one another and plastered. The natural umber, auburn or black of the vessels is not painted. New and old pieces are exhibited in the adjoining museum.

WICKERWORK

The *cestería* is a useful, hand-crafted item. The baskets are made from cane, straw, and the fibres of palm leaves, skilfully spliced and woven together by the craft workers.

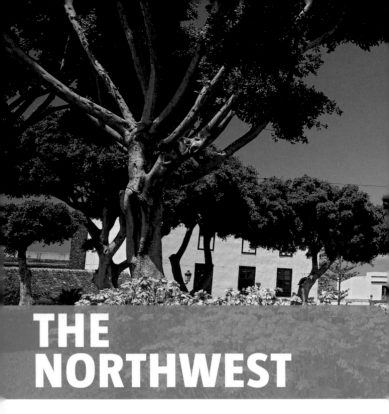

THE NORTHWEST

Nowhere else on Tenerife is the landscape more varied than in the northwest. The Valle de la Orotava is the green, fertile heart of the island. At one time this broad valley was the main settlement area for the Guanches, and the Spanish conquerors also preferred this bounteous region. First wine, then sugar cane and finally the banana brought prosperity to landowners.

When he first set eyes on the valley in 1799, Alexander von Humboldt is said to have fallen to his knees to thank God for creating this paradise. He later wrote: "... I have never beheld a prospect more varied, more attractive, more harmonious in the distribution of the masses of verdure and rocks than the western coast of Tenerife." A lookout point, the *Mirador de Humboldt* on the TF-21, has been created in his memory at the very spot where he surveyed the valley for the first time. Today, despite modest beaches and steep cliffs, tourism is the most important source of income. Boxy hotel blocks line the coastal zone around Puerto de la Cruz, the regional centre for the north of Tenerife. The further west you go, the more you put the tourist throng behind you. In small villages, farmers tend their crops, keep goats or cultivate vines, in much the same way as they have done for centuries, but always with an eye on Mount Teide looming behind them to the south. Stretching out beyond the town of Garachico are the rugged and largely uninhabited Teno Mountains. Until a few years ago the only human habitation

A region of contrasts – cultural heritage sites and holiday centres, barren volcanic slopes and lush vegetation

was in remote villages trapped in an almost medieval existence.

GARACHICO

(141 D2) *(∅ D5)* ☀ **Beautiful architecture, terrific nature – in ★ ☀ Garachico everything's still all right! Cobblestone alleys lined with historic buildings lead to a plaza with monasteries, churches and old bay laurels.**

Right behind, cliffs shoot up almost 1,000

m (3,330 ft), and on the lava coast, naturally formed pools offer a place to take a dip – but don't jump into the water unless it's calm! Garachico (pop. 5,700) is idyllic – but this didn't stop it from becoming the scene of a catastrophe: in 1706, mighty streams of lava erupted from the "Black Volcano" and flowed down across a broad front over the cliffs and into the sea, burying one of Tenerife's leading ports. But something new emerged: the hot lava cooled in the water of the Atlantic, where it conveniently formed new

Garachico's natural bathing spot: El Caletón

land, *Isla Baja,* or the "low island". The inhabitants defiantly rebuilt their new town on the only recently cooled lava. Taking a stroll through the Old Town, which still has some lovely buildings that miraculously survived the eruptions, is like being in a living museum.

SIGHTSEEING

EL CALETÓN
Want to go for a swim? The streams of lava that have cooled down in the sea are not only picturesque; they have also created natural bathing pools. When the sea is calm (but only then!), you can use the steps and metal ladders to climb down from the rocks into the sea for a swim.

CASTILLO DE SAN MIGUEL
Inconceivable, but true: this tiny castle once protected Garachico from pirate attacks. The portal, adorned with coats of arms, was built in 1575. Enter through it and imagine being on the "upper deck" of the fortificationand and expecting an enemy armada... *Daily 10am–6pm | admission 1.50 euros | Av. Tomé Cano*

CONVENTO DE SAN FRANCISCO
Here too we find ourselves transported back in time, to the year 1524. In this Franciscan monastery, you can walk like the monks once did through romantic cloisters and enter rooms with filigree stone flooring and artistic Mudéjar ceilings. But rather than relics, you'll now find natural history here. A relief model of Tenerife marks the locations of lava flows in recent centuries. And to allow visitors to visualise volcanic activity in general, multimedia installations show all of the earth's hotspots. Do you want to see more? The adjacent *Casa de la Cultura* presents different temporary (art) exhibitions. *Mon–Fri 10am–7pm, Sat, Sun 10am–3pm | admission 1 euro | Plaza de la Libertad*

IGLESIA DE SANTA ANA

The main church from 1520 is just three steps away from the convent. Here too, you'll find wooden Mudéjar ceilings, lava-stone pillars and dimly lit ambiance. The sorrowful and suffering saints at the main altar were carved by Luján Pérez, the Canaries' star sculptor in the 18th century. And take a look at the clock, which has been ticking with Swiss precision since time immemorial!

FOOD & DRINK

INSIDER TIP ARDEOLA

Take a seat on the sea promenade to enjoy creative Canarian cuisine in simple yet elegant surroundings. Ask Señor Ángel for the fish of the day! The restaurant's *milhoja de papas,* vegetable tartar sprinkled with goat's cheese, is particularly delicious. *Closed Mon; Tue, Wed evenings only | Av. Tomé Cano 4 | tel. 9 22 13 30 12 | www.restauranteardeola.com | Moderate*

CASA GASPAR

A nice, cosy address for years – meat from the grill and fresh fish, costed by weight, fast and friendly service. *Closed Sun, Mon | C/ Estebán del Ponte 44 | tel. 9 22 83 00 40 | Moderate*

PIZZERIA BACCO

A little restaurant opposite the pier offers homemade antipasti and the best pizza far and wide – all of it original and Italian! *Only Fri–Sun from 7pm | Av. de Venezuela 9 | mobile tel. 6 79 76 91 91 | Budget*

SHOPPING

ARTSHOP

Everything here is made by crafts-people and artists inspired by Tenerife: Guanche-style pottery, lava-stone jewellery and

pictures with island motifs. *C/ Estebán Ponte 3 | www.artshop-garachico.com*

CENTRO ARTESANÍA EL LIMONERO

Welcome to the kingdom of kitsch. Browse through "Canarian" handicrafts made in China, but with some local specialities, e.g. jam, cheese and wine. *Mon–Sat 10:30am–8:30pm, Sun 11am–7pm | Av. Tomé Cano 4 | www.casa-balcones.com*

WHERE TO STAY

LA QUINTA ROJA

Small, charming hotel in a renovated manor house on Garachico's most beautiful square. Shaded by palm fronds, you'll lose your sense of time in the patio with its bubbling fountain. Cosy rooms with lots of wood, breakfast on the garden terrace and roof terrace with jacuzzi and sauna to relax in. With a restaurant, cafeteria and *tasca* (wine bar), where even non-residents are welcome to hit the bottle. *Glorieta de San Francisco | tel. 9 22 13 33 77 | www.quintaroja.com | Moderate*

SAN ROQUE
A jewel in the crown of the Canarian hotel trade – this 17th-century mansion has been furnished with great attention to detail. All 20 rooms fitted out with designer furniture. Pool and terrace, not to mention the romantic leafy palio, create the perfect holiday atmosphere. *C/ Estéban de Ponte 32 | tel. 9 22 13 34 35 | www.hotelsanroque.com | Expensive*

WHERE TO GO

BUENAVISTA DEL NORTE
(140 B2) (*ᛗ C5*)
The name says it all: "buena vista" – good view – of rugged cliffs and the vast Atlantic! Tenerife's most westerly town (pop. 5,400) lies 10 km (7 miles) from Garachico. Towering up behind it are the impressive Teno Mountains. The TF-445 heads west to *Buenavista Golf (green fee: 1 round 75 euros | tel. 9 22 12 90 34 | www.buenavistagolf.es)*, an 18-hole golf course sloping down to the sea with the palatial five-star hotel *Hacienda del Conde (117 rooms | C/ La Finca | Tel. 9 22 06 17 00 | meliahaciendadelconde. com-tenerife.com | Expensive)*. Continue on the TF-445 past the ᛋ⅃ᛊ *Mirador de Don Pompeyo,* with a fine long-distance view, before it ends (risk of landslide if wet and windy) at the ᛋ⅃ᛊ *Punta de Teno*. An old lighthouse stands alongside the new one. On clear days the view extends as far as La Palma and La Gomera.

MACIZO DE TENO (TENO MOUNTAINS)
(140 B–C 3–4) (*ᛗ B–C6*)
Can you imagine that the Teno Mountains were once their own island? 7 million years ago, it rose from the sea floor and didn't become part of the "main island" around Teide until many more volcanic erruptions connected the two.
Even today, the 1,000 m (3,500 ft) high Teno Mountains seem remote and inaccessible: rugged gorges everywhere, steep cliffs and only the occasional green plateau. For centuries, the few villages here were practically cut off from the outside world. But since the early 1990s, an asphalt road, parts of which are still quite demanding for drivers, leads to this secluded corner of the island which today is protected as a *Parque Natural*. The ᛋ⅃ᛊ *Mirador de Cherfe* on the road from Santiago del Teide to Masca offers a great view of the world from atop rugged rocks.
If you love this wild, unspoilt terrain, keep going and then just south of El Palmar turn to the west toward *Teno Alto* (140 B3) (*ᛗ B6*). You pass a picnic site and then after 3 km (2 miles), you will reach this remote hamlet dispersed across a windswept upland plateau. Grazing on the pastures are goats and sheep, whose milk is processed into a ◉ cheese, which frequently wins awards. You can sample it in the bars on the church square, ideally with a glass of wine.

MASCA ★ ᛋ⅃ᛊ (140 B–C4) (*ᛗ C6–7*)
When you get close, you will barely notice this beautiful village in the middle of the Teno Mountains (situated some 21 km (13 miles) south of Garachico). The houses, spread across the hillsides, were built with blocks of stone hewn from the grey-brown rock found in the surrounding area. This architectural style is typical of the Teno region and Masca is the

best example. Until well into the 20th century, ancient shepherd tracks created by the Guanches were the only link with the outside world. They wound along the mountain slopes from village to village as far as Santiago del Teide. A leisurely way to get to know Masca is to visit either early in the morning or later on in the evening, when the place is not overrun by tourists on island coach tours. Below the main road you will find a number of a 🌿 tourist cafes, with terraces

Moderate), a museum-like estate from the year 1663. This is the perfect place for hikers that value comfort in old walls to spend the night. Two big historic wine presses at the entrance to the restaurant indicate: you can get good island wines here! Santiago manages the booming holiday towns around Los Gigantes, an inexhaustible goldmine for the municipality – but the wealth is scarcely visible... Are you interested in traditional handicrafts? Then the hamlet of Arguayo

An exceptional walking trail – through the Masca gorge down to the sea

overlooking the mountains and the valleys, e.g. *Casa Fidel (closed Thu | tel. 9 22 86 34 57 | Budget)*.

SANTIAGO DEL TEIDE (140 C4) *(𝄞 C7)*

On the way to the Teno Mountains you'll inevitably pass through Santiago. This town with its population of 5,400 is situated on a high plateau and has domed parish church. Right behind it, *La Casona del Patio (Av. de la Inglesia 72 | tel. 9 22 83 92 93 | lacasonadelpatio.com*

south of Santiago is just for you. It was once an important centre for Tenerife's pottery trade. Happily, the craft and the skills required live on in the **INSIDER TIP** *Museo del Alfarero (Tue–Sat 10am–1pm, 4pm–7pm, Sun 10am–2pm | admission free)*. The pottery museum is housed in a renovated workshop. Following the traditional Guanche method – i.e. no potter's wheel or tools – all ceramics are fired in an old oven. On sale here are the finished products, i.e. simple dishes, pots and pans in natural shades. The exhibits include some of the finest pieces the potters have produced and some old photographs from the days when business was booming.

LOS SILOS (140 C2) (*ɰ C5*)

A white "gingerbread"-style church on a plaza with a pavilion characterise the pleasantly sleepy centre of Los Silos (pop. 5,500, 6 km (4 miles) west of Garachico). Diagonally opposite the church in an old convent is a attractive visitors' centre. *The Centro de Visitantes (Mon–Fri 9am–1pm, Sat 9am–2pm | admission free | Plaza de la Luz 10)* can supply helpful information on the local geology, flora and fauna, and walking opportunities in the Teno Mountains. Walkers will find an excellent place to stay some 200 m (660 ft)from the coast. The outdoor holiday tour operator, Wikinger, runs a four-star aparthotel INSIDERTIP *Luz del Mar (35 rooms, 14 suites | Av. Sibora 10 | La Caleta | tel.*

9 22 84 16 23 | www.luzdelmar.de/englisch/st | *Moderate)* with large pool and spa. Guests will find here not only a wide choice of walking trails with detailed descriptions, but they will also have the opportunity to join in with (almost daily) guided tours. There are mountain bikes to hire and the centre also organises kayaking, caving and paragliding tours. In the evenings non-residents are welcome to eat in the adjoining *restaurant*, where there is a warm and friendly atmosphere. Many of the ingredients come from the ☘ organic finca that belongs to the centre. The road terminates right at the coast at ridiculously tall block of flats – a scar on a superb landscape. Owing to the lack of beaches, there is a swimming pool next door where you can go in for a dip. You won't be the only one looking longingly at the sea. There'll be a whale too. Or to be more precise, its original skeleton that was placed here – particularly unique landscape art.

ICOD DE LOS VINOS

(141 E2) (*ɰ E5*) **It's named after a tree and every year thousands of visitors flock here to admire it. But bear in mind that the legendary dragon tree in Icod de los Vinos is the finest example of its kind on the island.**

Although the ★ ● *Drago Milenario* does not date back a thousand years as the name suggests, its age is estimated at 500 to 600 years, and so must be the oldest dragon tree in the world. With an average trunk diameter of 6 m (20 ft) and a height of 17 m (56 ft), it is also unsurpassed in size. It occupies a prominent position in the middle of town within an enclosed garden, the *Parque del Drago (daily 9am–6pm | admission 5 euros | Plaza de la Constitución 1)*. The garden has in recent years been enlarged into a botanical garden with a collection of many native plants. There is also a Guanche trail, which sheds light on the lives of the island's aboriginal inhabitants.

But going for a stroll through Icod (pop. 23,000) can be fun too. Founded in 1501, it quickly acquired a reputation for its fertile vineyards. Many bodegas still line the streets and plazas of the Old Town.

SIGHTSEEING

IGLESIA SAN MARCOS & PLAZA DE PILA

Just a stone's throw away from the Drago Milenario stands the 15th-century *San Marcos* church on a romantic square. Through its Renaissance portal you'll enter into the dimly lit interior with its carved wooden ceiling. And don't forget to take a look at the silver-embossed Baroque altar! Even more silver lies in the Treasury. A few steps away from the church at Plaza de Pila, ringed by perfectly preserved town houses dating from the 18th century, you'll find a couple of nice shops where you can taste local wine.

INSIDERTIP MUSEO MUÑECAS / ARTLANDYA

Children's' dreams come true in this museum: hundreds of artist dolls designed by acclaimed designers are exhibited in an exotic hacienda. You can also find out how the dolls are made on an English-language guided tour of the workshop.. *Tue–Sun 10am–6pm | admission 10 euros | Camino el Moleiro 21 | Santa Bárbara | 3 km/1.9 miles to the east | www.artlandya.com*

FOOD & DRINK

CARMEN

It can get fairly cool in Icod. The perfect way to get warm is with a hearty soup,

A magnificent specimen – the Drago Milenario in Icod de los Vinos

e.g. the spicy cress stew, *potaje de berros*! And the rustic atmosphere with lots of wood will warm up your heart too. *Daily | C/ Hércules 2 | tel. 9 22 81 06 31 | Moderate*

WHERE TO STAY

INSIDERTIP SAN MARCOS

Are you looking for a small, historic and personal hotel? Then you're in the right place! Just below the church square, Domingo Toste lets six rooms in a stately home from the 18th century – all with period furniture, antique paintings and crystal chandeliers. The ☀ Superior room with a balcony and garden view is especially lovely. You can meet the other guests in the large, opulent salon, the airy patio or the former bodega. You can look forward to enjoying ⊕ excellent regional produce for breakfast! *C/ Hércules 11 | tel. 9 22 81 65 09 | www.sanmarcos-hotel.es | Moderate*

WHERE TO GO

CUEVA DEL VIENTO ● **(141 E3)** *(Ⓜ E6)*
If you want to climb into the bowels of a volcano, you're in the right place! First, at a small visitors' centre, you will receive an introduction into how the "cave of the wind" came into being. It was formed 27,000 years ago, when the Pico Viejo erupted and sent trails of lava flowing down into the valley. The lava cooled rapidly at the surface, while underneath it kept flowing, thereby creating tunnels; at 17 km (10 miles) in length, this is one of the longest lava tubes in the world. In eternal darkness, only highly adaptable creatures have been able to make a home here, including a blind cockroach – don't worry, it's totally harmless!
Only about 500 m (1,640 ft) of the cave is open to the public (there are plans to extend it to 1.8 km (1.1 miles)), but even this small section gives a good idea of the cave's dimensions and opens up vistas of lava lakes and galleries. *Tue–Sat 9am–4pm | admission 16 euros | visits (2 hrs) three times per day in Spanish and English for small groups | C/ los Piquetes 51 | pre-booking essential: tel. 9 22 81 53 39 | www.cuevadelviento.net | sturdy shoes required*

SAN JUAN DE LA RAMBLA
(142 A2) *(Ⓜ F5)*
It won't take long to walk through all the alleys of this historic, somewhat sleepy

town. More excitement can be found in the fishermen's quarter *Las Aguas* ("the waters"), where waves incessantly pound against the cliffs. It's not only nice to look at; it'll cause you to work up an appetite, which you can satisfy at ☀ Las Aguas restaurant *(closed Mon | C/ La Destila 20 | tel. 9 22 36 04 28 | Moderate)*, which occupies a country house above the promenade.

SAN MARCOS (141 E2) *(Ⓜ E5)*
One of the few beaches to swim at in the north, the INSIDER TIP *Playa de San Marcos* lies in a cove 2 km (1.2 miles) north of Icod. About 100 m (330 ft) in length, the beach of pitch-black volcanic sand is deserted on weekdays, but on Saturday and Sunday it fills up with hundreds of islanders, that come here to swim, spend the weekend in the nearby apartments and keep the small, local restaurants busy. One of them, ☀ *Casa María (daily | tel. 9 22 81 05 33 | Budget–Moderate)* is on the promenade overlooking sea and beach. Their speciality – like al-

Casas de los Balcones – wooden balconies surround the leafy inner courtyard of the Casa Fonseca

most everywhere else here – is fish.

LA OROTAVA

(142 C2) *(⌂ H5)* **Grand town houses line steep narrow lanes. Elegant mansions with spacious, dark-wood balconies surround large squares.**

Just ignore the cars and new housing developments on the outskirts – and you'll think you're back in colonial times! No wonder then that at the beginning of the 16th century the Spaniards decided to build a town here. Water bubbled from the many springs in the lushest part of the green *Valle de la Orotava*, its fertile soil providing bountiful harvests. They planted sugar cane, which they then shipped from the port, Puerto de la Orotava (now: Puerto de la Cruz), all over the world, and in the process amassed considerable wealth.

Although earthquakes in 1704 and 1705 destroyed large parts of the town, they were immediately rebuilt. That explains why the historic core remains largely intact and has been spared the architectural monstrosities of modern times. It is protected as a part of Europe's cultural heritage. Tourism in *La Orotava* (pop. 40,000) is mainly restricted to day visitors strolling through the Old Town with its fine squares. Thanks to attractive accommodation, you could stay here even longer...

SIGHTSEEING

CASAS DE LOS BALCONES ★

Several town houses of simple elegance face each other in *Calle San Francisco*. They get their name, *Casas de los Balcones*, from the wonderful finely turned wooden balconies, so typical of the Canaries. It's as if they have been stuck to the façade. The first, the *Casa Fonseca,* was built in 1632. What fascinates visitors is the tropical-green patio and an arcade panelled entirely with wood on the first floor. The rooms are now used by an embroidery school. On sale are blankets and fabrics, which you can watch being made. In 1670 the equally fine house next door, the *Casa de Franchi* was built; it now houses a carpet museum *(Museo de las Alfombras)*. However, these are not woven pieces, but floor coverings made from lava sand, as seen in the Corpus Christi celebrations. Opposite is *Casa Molina*, formerly a monastery dating from 1590. It now houses one of the island's largest craft shops. *www.casa-balcones.com*

CENTRO DE VISITANTES TELESFORO BRAVO DEL PARQUE

The national park information centre is where you need to go to get your permit to climb Mount Teide, but you can also learn a bit about its alpine flora there. And you can ☀ look out at the gigantic volcano from upstairs. *Tue–Sun 9am–2pm and 3:30pm–6pm | admission free | C/ Sixto Perera 25 | El Mayorazgo | junction 34 | tel. 9 22 92 23 71 | www.reservasparquesnacionales.es*

HIJUELA DEL BOTÁNICO

The "little daughter" (hijuela) of the *Puerto de la Cruz botanical garden* (see p. 46) is hidden behind the town hall, and at 4,000 m² (43,000 sq ft) ft, is indeed rather small. But it's still worth a visit. You can see Australian conifers, Indian chestnut trees, flame trees (flamboyants) and a lovely dragon tree. Some plants date back to the foundation of the garden in 1788. *Mon–Sat 9am–6pm | admission free | C/ Tomás Pére*

JARDINES DEL MARQUESADO DE LA QUINTA ROJA

Above the Hijuela del Botánico garden (see above), a pretty park climbs up the terraced slope. Passing by exotic plants competing with each other for the most magnificent colours, you will reach the ☀ **INSIDER TIP** *marble mausoleum* of the Marquis de la Quinta Roja and be able to enjoy a panorama of the city from above. *Daily 9am–6pm | admission free*

MUSEO DE ARTESANÍA IBEROAMERICANA

Within the walls of the former Dominican monastery of Santo Domingo, which dates from the 17th century, is an arts and crafts museum. You will see traditional costumes, instruments and beautiful everyday objects from Spain and the New World. The monastery's cloister is a masterpiece of simplicity. *Mon–Fri 10am–3pm | admission 3 euros | C/ Tomás Zerolo 34*

PARROQUIA DE LA INMACULADA CONCEPCIÓN DE LA VIRGEN MARIA

Less is more? Not here, where it's all about pomp! Two bell towers flank a massive, richly decorated Baroque façade. And that's just a taste of the splendour that awaits you inside. The three naves are divided by pillars and a mighty dome arches up over the crossing. It lets just enough light in to make the jasper and marble altar underneath shimmer mysteriously. In 1788, the Church of the Immaculate Conception was consecrated to the Virgin Mary. It was meant to surpass the beauty of its predecessor destroyed in the 1704-05 earthquakes: "What the destructive forces of nature take from us, we will rebuild all the more splendidly!" *Plaza Casañas*

PLAZA DEL AYUNTAMIENTO

La Orotava's main square, overlooked by seven towering Canary palm trees, is in front of town hall. This is the stage for all the major festivals, including the colourful Corpus Christi celebrations. In the weeks before Christmas, you can look at a beautiful life-sized nativity scene close by. *(C/ Isla de la Gomera 7)*

PLAZA DE LA CONSTITUCIÓN

Constitution Square centred around the café pavilion forms the heart of La Orotava. It is generously proportioned and always beautifully planted with flowers and shrubs. It is surrounded by a row of historical buildings – for example the *San Agustín* church, a former convent dating back to 1671, and the *Liceo de Taoro,* a palace painted in rust red which is now a private cultural centre. The view the plaza offers is great too: the town is at your feet!

RUTA DE LOS MOLINOS DE AGUA

No fewer than nine waterwheels were built to take advantage of La Orotava's abundance of water. Although built in the 16th century, they continued in use well into the 20th century.

They stood one behind the other along streets that climbed steeply up the hillside, their job being to grind *gofio*, the Canarian staple food. All were linked by channels, that carried water from the stream Araujo from one mill to another. Seven of the mills and parts of the channels can still be seen.

One of the three still functioning mills – in the *C/ Domingo González García 3* – is now powered by electricity and continues to grind *gofio*, which is sold there too. *Mon–Fri 8am–1pm and 3pm–7pm, Sat 8am–1pm | Start of route: south of the Casas de los Balcones*

FOOD & DRINK

SABOR CANARIO

"Canarian flavour" *(sabor canario)* in a historic estate in the Old Town. The chefs here devote loving attention to traditional fare – from *rancho* to *bienmesabe.* *Closed Sun | C/ Carrera 17 | tel. 9 22 32 27 25 | Budget–Moderate*

Meeting spot in La Orotava: the pretty café pavilion on the Plaza de la Constitución

SHOPPING

CASA DE LOS BALCONES AND CASA DEL TURISTA

As well as culinary specialities and tobacco products, the shops in the two houses opposite one another also sell *calados*, i.e. hemstitched embroidery, and *artesanía*, such as costumes, pottery and wood carvings. *Mon–Sat 9am–6:30pm (Casa de los Balcones also Sun) | C/ San Fernando 3 and 4*

CASA TORREHERMOSA

Certified (collector's) items made by Tenerife's artisans. Artenerife *(Mon–Fri 10am–3pm | C/ Tomás Zerolo 27)* is housed in a mansion built in the 17th century.

WHERE TO STAY

SILENE

This simple guesthouse offers comfortable accommodation in a town house. Three of the four rooms have balconies overlooking the town. *C/ Tomás Zerolo 9 | tel. 9 22 33 01 99 | Budget*

VICTORIA

This beautiful, two-storey mansion dating from the 16th century is now a lovely hotel with 14 rooms. A tiled, rustically furnished patio serves as a lounge, the in-house restaurant serves delicious food. Plus bar, tasca and sun terrace. *C/ Hermano Apolinar 8 | tel. 9 22 33 16 83 | www.hotelruralvictoria.com | Moderate*

INFORMATION

OFICINA DE TURISMO

C/ Calvario | tel. 9 22 32 30 41 | www.laorotava.es (sells the joint museum ticket)

WHERE TO GO

AGUAMANSA ☼ (142 C2) (𝟙 J5)

Beyond the village of Aguamansa, about halfway (10 km/7 miles) between La Orotava and the Parque Nacional del Teide, there is a dense pine forest. That is a good enough reason to take a break and look back up the Orotava Valley. Drive past the *Icona centre* in a house belonging to the National Park – where walkers will find a wealth of information – and you will find on the left-hand side the *La Caldera* picnic site in a volcanic crater. From there, signposted walking trails start in all directions.

PUERTO DE LA CRUZ

▨▨ MAP INSIDE BACK COVER
(142 B–C 1–2) (𝟙 G–H 4–5) **Large apartment blocks and hotels surrounded by lush gardens, colourful adventure pools, a rather rundown port, grand colonial buildings alongside neon-lit bars, bustling shopping streets, one end a haunt for old men passing the time of day on shady squares – this is Puerto de la Cruz in a nutshell. It's been difficult finding the right balance between the past, present and future, searching for a sound tourism concept for today and tomorrow.**

By 1900 the British had discovered this cool spot and pleasant climate, and claimed it for themselves. The first hotels were built in spacious gardens above the fishing village, which until then had been used by the Spanish, mainly as a port for exporting sugar cane and wine from the Orotava Valley. There were elegant hotels like the casino hotel Taoro, which still stands proudly above the city, but desperately needs investment. Many Canary islanders only settled here once tourism had become established; since the 1960s the spa hotels have been joined by multi-storey tourist blocks and guesthouses.

Puerto de la Cruz tries to meet the

CASA DE LA REAL ADUANA

One of the oldest buildings in Puerto de la Cruz is the Royal Customs House. Built in 1620, its wooden windows and balconies perfectly exemplify Canarian architecture. The last customs formalities were completed 150 years ago.

Today art and culture dominate behind the thick walls of the Castillo San Felipe

needs of its 45,000 inhabitants as well as meet the demands of the hundreds of thousands of holiday-makers who flock to the town. The locals and the world of tourism have to rub along together in this town, which has deep historic roots – that is what makes Puerto de la Cruz different from the resorts in the south. Between the Playa de Martiánez in the east and the Plaza del Charco in the centre, you will find many shops and restaurants, modern glass office buildings as well as examples of colonial architecture and squares to relax in.

Now the ground floor of the building houses the tourist office, an *Artenerife* shop selling handicrafts, kitchenware and local delicacies, while on display upstairs in the *Museum of Contemporary Art (MACEW)* are changing exhibitions of works by Canarian and other Spanish painters. *Mon–Fri 10am–5:30pm, Sat 10am–1pm | C/ Las Lonjas 1*

CASTILLO SAN FELIPE

Situated west of the town centre just under 1 km (0.6 miles) away is San Felipe castle. It was built between 1630 and

1644 to defend the island from pirates, hence the intimidating cannon outside the entrance. The building is now used for cultural events and exhibitions. There's a stunning view embracing the Playa Jardín. *Tue–Sat 11am–1pm and 5pm–8pm | admission free | Paseo de Luís Lavaggi*

IGLESIA DE NUESTRA SEÑORA DE LA PEÑA DE FRANCIA

Situated on the elevated Plaza de la Iglesia is Puerto's main church. The building was completed in 1697; however, the grey, neoclassical bell tower was added only 100 years ago. The heavily-gilded altarpiece on the Baroque main altar and several statues of saints, including the *Virgen del Rosario* and the *Virgen de los Dolores* create a remarkable spectacle. *C/ Quintana*

Spectacular: the large-leaved strangler fig in the Járdin Botánico

JARDÍN BOTÁNICO ★ ●

Cinnamon trees, sausage trees, strangler figs, pepper and tulip trees, coral and breadfruit trees, coffee and cocoa bushes, araucaria, various fruit trees and a fig tree as tall as a church – you can see all of this and much more at the Botanical Garden. In 1790, King Carlos III of Spain created it on 2.5 ha (6 acres) of land in 1790 to help exotic plants from the tropics to adjust to the temperate climate of Europe.

The second stage of this ambitious plan, i.e. to acclimatise the exotic plants on the Spanish mainland, did not succeed. Plants that flourished in tropical climates did not like the cool winters of Madrid. But the Botanical Garden has retained its importance and has evolved into an enchanted forest of unusual plants. *Daily 9am–6pm | admission 4.50 euros | C/ Retama 2*

MUSEO ARQUEOLÓGICO MUNICIPAL

On the west side of the Plaza del Charco stands the town's Archaeological Museum with Guanche mummies, weapons and historical maps. *Tue–*

The bars and restaurants around the Plaza del Charco are popular meeting-places at all times of day

Sat 10am–1pm and 5pm–9pm, Sun 10am–1pm | admission 2 euros (Thu free) | C/ del Lomo 9a

PARQUE TAORO ● ⚘

The first grand hotels for mainly British spa guests were built at the end of the 19th century on a plateau overlooking the sea and the town. The parkland covering 10 ha (25 acres) consists of gardens, footpaths, lookouts, waterfalls, fountains, a children's playground and a restaurant. Within the grounds behind the former Taoro Casino Hotel is a beautiful, terraced garden. Known as the Risco Bello, it boasts a fine array of beautiful flowers, plump fruits, an ivy-covered grotto and the water garden Jardin Acuático with its ponds. *Admission to the park free, Risco Bello 4 euros | Altos de Taoro*

PLAZA DEL CHARCO

Puerto de la Cruz's main square, the rectangular *Plaza del Charco*, is the place where the locals like to gather for a chat in the shadows of the Canary palms and Indian laurel trees. There's a playground for the children. Of particular note is the Rincón del Puerto, a building in Canarian style dating from 1739 with wooden balconies and a luxuriously planted patio, now shared by two restaurants.

PUERTO PESQUERO

Opposite the Plaza del Charco is the narrow fishing harbour. When the boats arrive back in port, buyers emerge amid a bustle of activity and the noisy haggling over the latest catch begins.

FOOD & DRINK

BAMBI GOURMET

Hidden away in a side street yet always well frequented: freshly made and varied Spanish dishes and Romanian (!) specialities in a cosy atmosphere. *Closed Sun | C/ Enrique Talg 15 | tel. 9 22 38 38 87 | www. bambi-gourmet.es | Moderate*

CASA RÉGULO

Imaginative, multiple award-winning Canarian cuisine in a renovated mansion. Do try the octopus carpaccio (*carpaccio de pulpo*)! *Closed Sun | C/ Pérez Zamora 16 | tel. 9 22 38 45 06 | Expensive*

EL DUENDE ●

Jesús Gonzalez is Tenerife's star chef and at the same time *el duende* or the "friendly spirit" of this house, playing with the colour and texture of his dishes. The menu showcases several creative dishes, e.g. a variation of the *Tinerfeño* favourite, *costillas con papas* (ribs with potatoes): at the bottom of a cocktail glass is minced meat, on top sweetcorn, potato foam and a dab of coriander mojo. *Closed Mon, Tue | La Higuerita 41 | motorway junction 38, then follow signs to La Vera (TF-320) | tel. 9 22 37 45 17 | Expensive*

EL TALLER SEVE DÍAZ

"Seve's workshop" is a small, elegant restaurant in Puerto's food district. First of all, you'll be met by a free welcome from the kitchen and homemade bread, followed by creative Canarian dishes that will delight both your eyes and your palate. Ideal for a special evening! *Wed-Sun 7pm–10:30pm, Sat, Sun also 1–3pm | C/ San Felipe 32 | tel. 8 22 25 75 38 | Moderate-Expensive | tasting menu approx. 40 euros*

INSIDER TIP EL TEMPLO DEL VINO

A culinary and wine-tasting paradise: exquisite Canarian-Spanish wines served with delicious tapas. *Closed Tue | C/ del Lomo 2 | tel. 9 22 37 41 64 | www. templodelvino.com | Moderate*

SHOPPING

CALLE QUINTANA

You'll find everything – from art gallery to supermarket – in the pedestrian zone in the heart of the Old Town. Take a look around the *Columbus Plaza* shopping centre with its attractive patio – there are shops selling everything from the latest fashions to cigars and perfumes.

MERCADO MUNICIPAL

The concrete market hall is not a pretty sight. But it still attracts many shoppers looking for fresh fruit and vegetables, fish and meat. If you're craving whole-grain bread and good cake, visit *Harry's Gourmeteria* upstairs. There is also a flea market here on Wednesdays and Saturdays from 10am to 2pm. *Mon–Sat 8am–2pm and 4–8pm | C/ Blas Pérez González 6 | www.mercadopuertodelacruz.es*

INSIDER TIP MUNDO DEL MAPA

Do you need a hiking map? Or how about a book on Tenerife? Near the Plaza del Charco, the hub of Puerto de la Cruz, Antonio and Verena will help you find the perfect island reading material. They also sell a few items to make hiking easier, e.g. trekking poles and torches, aloe vera sunscreen and dried fruit as trail mix. Hiking trips can be booked here as well. *C/ San Felipe 12*

BEACHES

INSIDER TIP PLAYA DE BOLLULLO

Hidden away beneath a picturesque range of steep cliffs not far to the east of Puerto de la Cruz lies this 200 m (650 ft) long, pitch-black beach. For refreshments, there is also a beach bar.

PLAYA DE MARTIÁNEZ ☼

The almost untouched town beach (250 m (820 ft) in length) to the east of Puerto de la Cruz is composed of coarse, black sand with outcrops of volcanic rock. A boardwalk has been laid for walkers. Plus there's an incredible view along the north coast. Restaurants and cafeterias are all along the 1 km (0.6 mile) long *playa*. The brightly coloured tropical flowers lend the beach its charm.

PLAYA JARDÍN

Huge quantities of dark sand were required to create this "garden beach" to the west of Puerto de la Cruz. To ensure that all the sand does not get swept away, tons of rocks were dumped in the sea to create an artificial offshore reef. Good showers and toilets provided.

SPORTS & LEISURE

If you prefer to get around Puerto de la Cruz by bicycle, you can hire mountain bikes opposite the bus station from 65 euros for 3 days at *MTB Active (C/ Puerto Viejo 44/Dr Madan (next to the San Borondón hotel) | mobile tel. 6 69 15 75 67 (9–11am) and 6 20 00 59 98 (4:30–6:30pm) | www.mtb-active.com)*.

ENTERTAINMENT

Plaza del Charco is a popular spot, with bars, cafés and ice cream parlours. *Dinámico (open daily)* on the square is an open-sided pavilion with a large bar, lots of tables and a good selection of drinks and snacks.

At the weekend there's Latin American and Spanish live music along with good food in the rustic *Bodega Julián (C/ Mequinez 20 | mobile tel. 6 86 55 63 15 | Moderate)* just around the corner.

Night owls will inevitably find themselves heading towards Lago de Martiánez. *Café de Paris (Av. de Colón 2)* with a terrace serves cocktails until midnight. Only after midnight and at weekends do things get lively in *Calle La Hoya* and the intersecting *Av. Familia Bethencourt y Molina*.

For a more sedate form of relaxation, above Puerto de la Cruz is *Abaco (C/ Casa Grande | Urbanización El Durazno | tel. 9 22 37 01 07 | www.abacotenerife. com)*, a superbly-restored country estate, which you can also visit during the day *(Tue–Sun 10am–1:30pm folklore shows | admission 9 euros)*. In the evening you can enjoy exotic (high-priced) cocktails at the bar, convivial seating areas in the

Playa Jardín: the black sandy beach of Puerto de la Cruz lies at the foot of the Teide

rooms or wicker chairs in the romantic gardens. Classical concerts performed by small ensembles and flamenco shows regularly take place in the evening.

If your holiday cash is running out, then you can always take a chance at the casino *(Mon–Wed and Fri 8pm–4am, Sun and Thu 8pm–3am| admission free (remember your passport) | tel. 9 22 38 05 50 | www.casinostenerife.com)*. It is situated in the pool area by Lago de Martiánez and has a restaurant, a pub and a snack bar.

WHERE TO STAY

LAS AGUILAS ⚘

This aparthotel perched high above the town boasts splendid all-round views. Idyllic location and very quiet. Some 219 suite-like units. Family-friendly mini-club with pool and playground. Beach a short distance away, but shuttle-bus available. *C/ Doctor Barajas 19 | tel. 9 22 37 28 06 | www.hotellasaguilas.com | Moderate*

BAHÍA PRÍNCIPE SAN FELIPE ⚘

The all-inclusive hotel has a fine location on the seafront with a view of the Orotava Valley and Mount Teide. **INSIDER TIP** Get in early and book the corner double rooms with panoramic terrace. Several pools, spa, fitness suite. Good à la carte restaurants. 261 rooms | *Av. Colón 22 | tel. 9 02 10 03 60 | www.bahia-principe.com | Moderate–Expensive*

BOTÁNICO

Five-star hotel with its own gardens, lakes and sub-tropical feel. Grandiose architectural style and lots of marble may be a little anachronistic, but the 250 large, luxuriously-appointed rooms and the exquisite service really are top-class. Gardens with terraces, pools and lawns brighten the complex.

Guests can use the facilities of the exclusive *Oriental Spa Garden* free of charge, and the hotel has four restaurants and a bar. *C/ Richard J. Yeoward 1 | tel. 9 22 38 14 00 | www.hotelbotanico. com | Expensive*

MONOPOL

The beautiful, 250-year-old hotel in Canarian style is situated in the heart of Old Town and boasts a patio with arcades and new annexe. *92 rooms,* **INSIDER TIP** when booking if possible request one of the 35 rooms in the old block | *C/ Quintana 15 | tel. 9 22 38 46 11 | www.monopoltf.com | Budget–Moderate*

PUERTO AZUL

For travellers: the small, friendly hotel in a pedestrian lane in the Old Town offers 26 rooms with a balcony. If you want to learn Spanish, you're in the right place; there's a language school right in the building. *C/ del Lorno 24 | Tel. 9 22 38 32 13 | www.puerto-azul.com |*

TIGAIGA TENERIFE ⚘

Smart mid-range hotel with 83 rooms (ask for **INSIDER TIP** west-facing room if you want a view of Mount Teide). In a tranquil setting in Taoro Park with terraced garden, pool and a gorgeous view of sea and mountains. *Parque Taoro 28 | tel. 9 22 38 35 00 | www.tigaiga.com | Moderate–Expensive*

INFORMATION

OFICINA DE TURISMO

C/ Las Lonjas/Casa de Aduana | Tel. 9 22 38 60 00 | www.tenerife.es

LOS REALEJOS (142 A–B2) *(🗺 G5)*
Situated some 5 km (3 miles) west of Puerto de la Cruz is the municipality of several comfortable houses particularly popular with families. Children can run around freely, play with the animals and try the exotic homegrown (organic) fruits. The farm has its own

The Iglesia de Nuestra Señora de la Concepción in the picturesque Los Realejos

Los Realejos (pop. 36,000), an amalgamation of a number of smaller settlements. They are spread out over steep ridges separated by deep water canyons. Tenerife's first church (1496) consecrated Santiago Ápostol, is testimony to the community's former wealth and has now been taken over by the hotel next door.

A treasure for individualists is 🌄 **INSIDER TIP** *Finca el Quinto (Caserío los Quintos 37 | tel. 9 22 34 50 02 | www.fincaelquinto.de/en | Budget)*. This finca is situated on an enormous estate on the edge of the *Castro National Reserve* high above the sea. The Köllmann family runs an organic farm and offers accommodation in

fresh water source and serves eggs from their own hens for breakfast. No artificial fertilisers are used.

The restaurant *El Monasterio (daily | La Vera | C/ La Montaña | tel. 9 22 34 07 07 | www.mesonelmonasterio.com | Budget–Moderate)* occupies the premises of a former monastery in La Montañeta, close to Puerto de la Cruz. Small animals roam freely in the grounds, which are beautifully landscaped with plenty of greenery. Guests can choose between typical Canarian cuisine in the superb restaurant or light snacks in the cafeteria.

THE NORTHEAST

The Cumbre Dorsal mountains separate Tenerife's two coasts like a backbone, climbing steadily towards Mount Teide in the southwest; at the other end in the northeast there are the largely inaccessible Montañas de Anaga. Only two winding roads lead up into this 1,000 m (3,300 ft) high range.

Tenerife's more recent history started in the northeast. This is where the Spanish came ashore and fought with the Guanches. They suffered defeats and celebrated important victories, which shaped the island's fortunes later on. The development of the region was also influenced by its geography, which could only support limited habitation. Farming families still live in narrow gorges and hidden coves, leading lives which follow an almost medieval pattern based around work in the fields and the extended family. That is what life is like in villages just beyond the suburbs of the capital, Santa Cruz de Tenerife, a bustling metropolis where liberal Mediterranean values prevail. At the flattest point of the Cumbre Dorsal lies La Laguna, where in colonial times the leading figures in the church and the state resided. Since Unesco awarded it World Heritage Site status, there has been considerable investment, and the city is now finer than ever.

Settlements along the fertile northwest coast spread from La Laguna. Tenerife's "grain store" is also the largest vine-growing region in the Canaries. And the region grows much more than that – everything from fruit and potatoes to flowers. Unfortunately, the impact of tourism

A busy city and wooded uplands – from metropolitan Santa Cruz it's just a short hop to the almost unspoilt Anaga Mountains

is highly visible. Large areas of this often rugged, picturesque coast have fallen victim to a building boom.

BAJAMAR & PUNTA DEL HIDALGO

(138 B1–2) (*L–M 1–2*) **Bajamar and Punta del Hidalgo are quiet re-**

sorts popular with summer visitors. Built high but at low cost during the 1960s, the two places are currently undergoing a facelift.

Bajamar boasts a promenade and two large, ● *free natural swimming pools,* where salt water is circulated straight from the sea. There is also a natural swimming pool in Punta del Hidalgo. From there, you can walk about 4 km (2.5 miles) along the coast, past the lighthouse to the "Two Brothers" (see *Chinamada*) – two cliffs at the base

The Catedral Santa Iglesia in La Laguna

of the Anaga range. For people who generally shun tourists, both places make a good holiday alternative.

FOOD & DRINK

COFRADÍA DE PESCADORES

Go for a swim in the natural pool at Punta del Hidalgo, then enjoy some fish in this restaurant run by the fishermen's association – preferably at sunset! *Daily | Av. Marítima 46 | Punta del Hidalgo | tel. 9 22 15 69 54 | Budget–Moderate*

INSIDER TIP EL LEÓN
COCINA NATURAL

Just as fresh and cheerful as the atmosphere is the charismatic hostess Macarena. In her small restaurant, she offers vegetarian and vegan food as well as an inexpensive lunch menu and organic Tenerife wines. Diabetics can look forward to sugar-free desserts. The food is guaranteed to leave you feeling full and happy! *Daily, Mon–Wed, Sun only for lunch | Av. del Sol 13 | Bajamar | mobile tel. 6 90 95 73 41 | Budget*

WHERE TO STAY

INSIDER TIP OCÉANO ☆

Relax and have a good time. Each of the 78 bright apartments have a large balcony with sea view. The spa is excellent offering four saunas and a thalasso pool. Go past the garden pool to reach the hotel's natural swimming pool with its rippling waves. Its staff and healthy food are rated highly; the hotel also employs a team of doctors and therapists to look after the well-being of its guests. Impressive program of cultural events and activities. Fantastic walks set off right at the hotel's front door! *C/ Océano Pacifico 1 | Punta del Hidalgo | tel. 9 22 15 60 00 | www.oceano.de | Moderate*

WHERE TO GO

CHINAMADA (138 C2) (*M1–2*)

The TF-13 coast road peters out in Punta del Hidalgo. At the end there's an ☆ impressive view over the north coast and the *Roque de los Dos Hermanos,* the Rock of the Two Brothers. Starting below the bend is a waymarked INSIDER TIP hiking trail (10 km/7 miles, about 3 hours) to Chinamada, a pretty village noted for its cave dwellings. Carved out of the tufa rock, the houses have white-washed facades.

CITY **WHERE TO START?**
Whether you arrive by car, bus or tram, your first stop really ought to be the city's historic centre. The best place to start an exploratory tour of the city is the **Plaza del Adelantado**. This is where you will find the tourist information office where you can book free guided tours of the city.

LA LAGUNA

(138 B3) *(🕮 M3)* **Do you want to stroll through historic streets, visit venerable monastery courtyards and stop for a bite in rustic bodegas? La Laguna, a Unesco world heritage site, is ideal for a day trip, and even for a longer stay.**

But few people want to spend their entire holiday here, because up on the plateau, it can get cool and cloudy – after all, the town is stuck right in the middle of the trade wind clouds at an elevation of 500 m (1,600 ft). What is now a nightmare for holidaymakers was once a blessing for settlers. The moist cool air ensures bountiful harvests: first for the Guanches, then for the Spanish conquerors. It's not surprising that they made La Laguna the island's first capital in 1496.

It wasn't long before the town had become the archipelago's intellectual centre. In 1701 the first university in the Canary Islands was founded here. Although in 1723 it lost political power to the emerging town of Santa Cruz, with its university and an episcopal seat, La Laguna remains the cultural heart of Tenerife and it continues to be a vibrant city of 135,000 inhabitants. Its colonial legacy is still evident and nurtured, as is reflected in the many fine buildings in Canarian style.

SIGHTSEEING

CATEDRAL SANTA IGLESIA

Tenerife's cathedral was built in the 20th century on the ruins of the first church which dates back to 1511. Many works of art are preserved from this time, including expressive sculptures by the Canarian artist José Luján Pérez. *Plaza Fray Albino*

IGLESIA DE NUESTRA SEÑORA DE LA CONCEPCIÓN

IIt's worth a look inside La Laguna's oldest church (1496) for the painted wooden ceiling, a magnificently carved Baroque pulpit and a baptismal font brought by the Spanish conqueror Alonso Fernández de Lugo. From the tall bell

MARCO POLO HIGHLIGHTS

★ **Cumbre Dorsal**
A tour along the "backbone of Tenerife" passes through a varied range of lands → p. 58

★ **Auditorio de Tenerife**
An architectural masterpiece became the symbol of the island → p. 60

★ **Palmetum**
Palm tree park on a former landfill → p. 61

★ **Tenerife Espacio de las Artes**
Santa Cruz's art centre is a feast for the eyes both inside and out → p. 63

★ **Playa de las Teresitas**
At weekends this gem of a beach attracts thousands of *Tinerfeños* → p. 65

tower next to the church you can enjoy a fine view of the town and the highlands. *Mon 10am–2pm, Tue–Fri 10am–5pm | C/ Obispo Rey Redondo*

MUSEO DE LA CIENCIA Y EL COSMOS ●

The Museum of Science and the Cosmos with its planetarium is recognisable from afar, mainly because of its huge radio telescope. At over 70 different "stations", you can learn about the complicated connections between the earth, sun, solar system, Milky Way and about human existence in an interactive and fun way. *Tue–Sun 9am–8pm, Sun, Mon 10am–5pm | admission 5 euros | Av. Los Menceyes 70 | www.museosdetenerife.com*

MUSEO DE HISTORIA DE TENERIFE

Even if you're not interested in Canarian history, this palace dating from 1593 is worth a visit! The patio with its richly carved wooden gallery is a fine example of colonial architecture: *Casa de Lercaro (Tue–Sat 9am–8pm, Sun, Mon 10am–5pm | admission 5 euros | C/ San Agustín 22 | www.museosdetenerife.com).* In the ● Fundación Cristino de Vera (admission free) a few doors further on you can admire the nearly 100 paintings by the Tenerife-born painter of the same name.

FOOD & DRINK

LA BOURMET

Over ten different gourmet burgers, fried sweet potatoes and homemade bread served with island beers and wines. *Closed Mon | C/ San Agustín 42 | tel. 9 22 25 04 13 | www.labourmet.com | Budget*

LA MAQUILA

Warm up with *conejo en salmorejo* (rabbit in a spicy marinade) and a glass of red wine. Cheap lunch menu. *Closed Tue | Callejón de Maquila 4 | tel. 9 22 25 70 20 | Moderate*

TAPASTÉ ☺

Restaurant recommended for vegetarians and vegans; everything here is homemade, organic and regional. They don't use preservatives or food colouring, and white sugar is taboo. The alternating three-course menus cost about 10 euros. *Mon–Sat 1–4pm | Plaza San Cristóbal 37 | tel. 8 22 01 55 28 | tapaste.es | Budget*

EL TIMPLE

Ana is in charge of the kitchen, while her husband Benito alternates between kitchen and dining room. Most *Tinerfeños* order a *ración* (portion) – and because home cooking tastes so good, they can't resist a second one. *Closed Sun, Mon | C/ Candilas 4 | tel. 9 22 25 02 40 | Moderate*

SHOPPING

The traffic-calmed streets are lined with both small groceries and trendy boutiques. For good wines from Tenerife seek out *Viña Norte (Plaza de la Concepción 16),* for handicrafts ranging from pottery and textiles to basketry, try *Atlántida (San Agustín 55 | atlantidaartesania.es).* At *Valleverde (C/ Ascanio y Nieve 6 | www.valleverde-canarias.com)* you can find up-to-date outdoor equipment – from trekking poles to hiking shoes.

ENTERTAINMENT

One bodega after another on the pedestrian streets *C/ Herradores* and *C/ Obispo Rey Redondo.* There are also many bars

There are good views of the Pico del Teide from the Cumbre Dorsal

to the south of Plaza del Adelantado towards the university district.

WHERE TO STAY

AGUERE
Located between the two main churches, this small hotel occupies a former palace building. The 23 rooms are furnished with antiques, and there is a cosy, glass covered patio with a café. *C/ La Carrera 55 | tel. 9 22 31 40 36 | www.hotelaguere.es | Budget*

CASA EL PORTE
Some 3 km (2 miles) from La Laguna, in the tiny village of *Portezuelo,* Ana de Armas has transformed her ancestral home into colourful, rustic-style accommodation with a large garden where orange and medlar trees flourish. The *casa* consists of two residential units for three or four people, each with its own terrace. *www.turismorural.de | Moderate*

INSIDER TIP LAGUNA NIVARIA HOTEL & SPA
The most beautiful hotel in the most beautiful spot. This hotel owes its four stars to its traditional palace architecture, its cosy apartments and its spa, where you can relax after sightseeing. The café and restaurant are popular haunts for Laguneros. *73 rooms and apartments | Plaza del Adelantado | tel. 9 22 26 42 98 | www.lagunanivaria.com | Moderate–Expensive*

INFORMATION

OFICINA DE TURISMO
Housed in a splendid building, the centre provides lots of useful information. Free city tours start here Mondays to Fridays at 11:30am. *C/ Obispo Rey Redondo 7 | tel. 9 22 63 11 94 | www.turismolalaguna.com*

LA LAGUNA

The houses of the village of Taganana climb up the slopes around the edge of the Anaga Mountains.

WHERE TO GO

CUMBRE DORSAL ★
(142–143 B–F 1–4) (*M G–L 4–6*)

The 42-km (26-mile) journey along the narrow mountain ridge from La Laguna to Teide National Park is the best trip you could ever make in a car on Tenerife. Passing through a kaleidoscope of varied landscapes, the road climbs to a height of 2,300 m (7,500 ft). To the west of the old capital, cacti and orange trees bask on the arid plateau, at the centre of which is *La Esperanza*, a neat, if rather sleepy, village. Esperanza Forest begins higher up. Dense pine forests and tall eucalyptus keep the soil cool, ferns find shade, laurel and pine plantations will hopefully make up for centuries of felling. You will find it hard to resist the tasty home cooking, if you stop by at the rustic-style **INSIDER TIP** *Las Raíces* restaurant in the heart of the forest *(closed Mon | Budget)*. From the *Mirador Montaña Grande* at 1,120 m (3,675 ft), you can see La Palma, on the other side Gran Canaria. Entry into

the cloud forest can often be abrupt. At the *Mirador de Ortuño*, Mount Teide, often snow-capped in winter, comes into view. In summer, the seven red watchtowers, one of which is visible on the left, are manned around the clock – forest fires are the biggest threat to this region. At 2,000m (6,600ft) the road reaches the tree line. The rocks are craggy, stocky pines, gorse bushes and low shrubs withstand the often harsh winds and wide temperature fluctuations. Jagged ridges of lava, along with black, leaden and red fields of ash, are evidence of volcanic eruptions that took place millions of years ago. Just past the white towers of the Observatory, you will reach the Centro de Visitantes El Portillo (see p. 71), the National Park's Information Centre and the start of the lunar landscape surrounding Mount Teide.

MONTAÑAS DE ANAGA
(138–139 B–E2) (*M L–P2*)

Northeast of Santa Cruz and La Laguna, roads that get increasingly tortuous wind

were out of reach even to the Spanish settlers, who from the outset indiscriminately felled the island's forests. In many places the woodland is interspersed with bizarre tree heath (Erica arborea) – large trees, from whose branches hang long strands of lichen. Like sponges they absorb the moisture from the trade wind clouds, which ascend in dense swathes. If the mist clears, the *miradores*, viewing points, afford great long-distance views. The sweeping view from the highest, ❄ *Pico del Inglés* (992 m/3,255 ft), takes in the Atlantic surf at Punta del Hidalgo and the beach at Las Teresitas. At the Mirador Cruz del Carmen, marked hiking trails wind through rugged mountain terrain. For a leaflet about it call in at the **INSIDER TIP** *visitor's centre* (*daily 9:30am–4pm*). You can regain your strength with dishes made using regional ingredients at Bistro *La Gangochera* (*daily | tel. 9 22 26 42 12 | Budget*), opposite the visitor's centre.

into the cool Anaga Mountains. For millions of years the laurel forest has survived in this remote area, where there is still very little habitation. These steep inclines

FOR BOOKWORMS AND FILM BUFFS

Óscar – una pasión surrealista – international co-production by Lucás Fernández about the life of the Canarian painter, Óscar Domínguez, a contemporary and friend of Pablo Picasso. Many of his paintings are in the TEA in Santa Cruz.

The Clash of the Titans – starring Liam Neeson and Ralph Fiennes, features the landscapes of Tenerife (2009).

Jason Bourne – Paul Greengrass shot the fifth part of the Jason Bourne series in 2016, leading actor was Matt Damon. Tenerife was the film location chosen to illustrate places in Beirut as well as the airports of Athens and Reykjavík. The Plaza de España in Santa Cruz de Tenerife represented Syntagma Square in Athens.

The Deadliest Plane Crash – in 1977 two fully loaded 747 jumbo jets collided at Los Rodeos airport killing 583 people – the full story (DVD/1997).

More Ketchup Than Salsa: Confessions of a Tenerife Barman – Joe Cawley, a British expat in business on Tenerife, takes a light-hearted look at life on the island (Kindle/2005).

The largest village in the range is *Taganana* (139 D2) (*Ⓓ N2*), which lies in a broad valley beneath a backdrop of tall mountain peaks. The triple-nave church of *Nuestra Señora de las Nieves,* which dates from 1506, houses a valuable Flemish-style triptych from the same period. Down by the wild surf of the coast, you'll find the hamlets of *Roques de la Bodega* and *Benijo* with their fish restaurants. If you stay up on the ridge, you'll reach the ⚲ *Mirador El Bailadero* with its panoramic view over the village. Nearby is the INSIDER TIP *Albergue Montes de Anaga (tel. 9 22 82 20 56 | www. alberguestenerife.net | Budget)* with nine double rooms and dorms, the ideal overnight stop for hikers and bikers.

SANTA CRUZ DE TENERIFE

MAP INSIDE BACK COVER
(138 C4) (*Ⓓ M–N 3–4*) **Tenerife's capital rises back from the coast towards the jagged mountains in a series of terraces; in the city sober apartment blocks and stately colonial buildings stand together in perfect harmony.**

Although Santa Cruz (pop. 230,000) is a lively port, the pace is leisurely. Large parts of the city are either traffic calmed or pedestrian zones. Pavement bars and cafés are firmly in local hands, Canarian laissez-faire is the order of the day.

In 1494 the Spaniard Alonso Fernández de Lugo landed in the bay and established the first settlement here. Santa Cruz was initially overshadowed by La Laguna, 5 km (3 miles) inland, but it has been the seat of Tenerife's government since 1723. Commercially important for the city is the sprawling port, where goods from all over the world are traded.

SIGHTSEEING

AUDITORIO DE TENERIFE ★
The snow-white concert hall is a daring building designed by Spain's star architect, Santiago Calatrava. Its most striking feature is the trio of huge, shell-shaped wings arcing over the auditoria, giving the building an airborne, almost weightless appearance. But not only is it visually impressive, the acoustics are also extraordinarily good. Every week INSIDER TIP concerts in all musical genres, as well as opera and ballet, are held in the bright and airy halls. Tours of the building are also available (ask at the tourist information office for times). *Av. de la Constitución | www.auditoriodetenerife.com*

IGLESIA DE NUESTRA SEÑORA DE LA CONCEPCIÓN
The slender bell tower for the oldest church (1502) in Santa Cruz was built in typical colonial style and for many years served as an important landmark for sailors. After a fire, the triple-nave church with its many side chapels underwent several restorations during the 17th and 18th centuries. Slim volcanic stone columns support the building internally. Precious Baroque works of art include a high altar, a coloured marble

> **CITY WHERE TO START?**
> The **bus station (Estación Central de Guaguas)** is situated south of the city centre. From here it's easy to reach the market *(mercado)* and the TEA Arts Centre in the Old Town. If you are arriving by car, then look for a car-park close to the **Plaza de España** and then start your city tour here.

pulpit, paintings, gold and silver treasures and the "Holy Cross of the Conquest" dating from 1494. *Av. Bravo Murillo*

IGLESIA DE SAN FRANCISCO/ MUSEO DE BELLAS ARTES

The Franciscan monks have long since left Santa Cruz. Their monastery has

follow the traces of the island's history. You'll be there to experience Tenerife's volcanic formation and learn how plants developed on what was once barren lava. Then you'll meet the first settlers, the Guanches. Their preserved skulls are neatly lined up in glass cases. Tools, ornaments and everyday objects belonging to the early Canarian

A striking combination: the extravagant shell-shaped concert hall set against the pool

been turned into an art museum with works by Dutch and Spanish but especially Canarian masters. But the church still serves the Lord. Dive into its sacred atmosphere with volcanic pillars, Baroque altars and carved wood ceilings. *Church: Plaza San Francisco | Museum: Tue–Fri 10am–8pm, Sat, Sun 10am–2pm | admission free | C/ José Murphy 12*

MUSEO DE LA NATURALEZA Y EL HOMBRE ●

In a former hospital, a magnificent building in the style of classicism, you'll

population complete the picture. *Tue–Sun 9am–8pm, Mon 10am–5pm | admission 5 euros | C/ Fuente Morales | www.museosdetenerife.org*

PALMETUM ★

Where thousands of tonnes of rubbish were once rotting away, a botanical garden was built: 111 ha (27 acres) and full of palm trees from all over the world. Labyrinthine paths will lead you over little hills, past ponds and waterfalls. Sensitive exotic tropical plants, which will be planted in the wild one day, are cultivated in the greenhouse. *Daily 10am–6pm, last admission 1 h before closing | admission 6 euros | Av. de la Constitución | palmetumtenerife.es*

PARQUE GARCÍA SANABRIA

A great place to catch your breath. Stroll

Bright: the reading room at the Tenerife Espacio de las Artes

down wide paths, past enormous trees and exotic flowers. Here and there, you'll run into sculptures, arcades and fountains – with dreamlike squares for you sit for a breather. You can also get something to eat or drink at the well-visited *cafeteria* at the (lower) entrance to the park.

PLAZA DE ESPAÑA & PLAZA DE LA CANDELARIA

The broad Plaza de España with its gigantic circular pool of water, many trees and floating tropical lamps is very attractive. Its fountain shoots a jet of water skywards every hour. Two unassuming pavilions overgrown with plants stand behind the square, home to the tourist information centre and a crafts shop run by Artenerife. The residence of the island's government administration, *Cabildo Insular,* towers over the other side of the square; an electric nativity scene is erected here in December which attracts many visitors.

Near the Cabildo stands the massive memorial to the soldiers who died during the Civil War. Giant athletic warriors sporting swords and helmets, reminiscent of German Nazi art, commemorate those who fought and died for the dictator Franco. You can get away from the monstrous sight by (literally) sinking into the ground. Through an unobtrusive entryway, you can descend into the underground foundations of the *Castillo de San Cristóbal fortress (Mon–Sat 10am–6pm | admission free)*. It was erected in 1575 to fend off pirates and in 1928 – long since useless – razed to make room for the expanding city. In the twilight, well suited to Santa Cruz's basement, you can see displays on all of the city's fortifications. There's even a replica of the famous "El Tigre" cannon, which routed Admiral Nelson in 1797, to commemorate the military history of the city.

Further inland lies the adjacent Plaza de la Candelaria. The "bearer of light" floats on top of a tall, white Carrara marble column – the Virgin of Candelaria is Tenerife's patron saint. Santa Cruz's shopping district begins at Plaza de la Candelaria, with an eclectic mixture of trendy and traditional shops.

PLAZA DEL PRÍNCIPE ASTURIAS

A magnificent square named after the

son of the Spanish king. Mature trees and lush vegetation create the impression of a sub-tropical oasis.

LA RAMBLA

This long boulevard arcs around the centre of the city. Kiosks and benches shaded by tall trees line the pedestrian walkway in the centre. Modern sculptures – including ones by Henry Moore and Joan Miró – bring art into everyday life. The old bull-ring halfway round is now only used for sporting events and pop concerts.

TENERIFE ESPACIO DE LAS ARTES ★

Tenerife's ambitious art and cultural centre. Externally, this elongated complex fits perfectly into the *barranco*, the long ravine, which runs through the city towards the coast. Inside, strictly angled lines, tall glass façades and an open patio allow plenty of light in. A permanent exhibition displays the life's work of the great Tenerife-born surrealist Óscar Domínguez. Alongside it are temporary exhibitions of international contemporary art movements. There is also a large library and a nice cafeteria. *Plus 36 internet terminals available free of charge. Tue–Sun 10am–8pm | admission 5 euros | Av. de San Sebastián 10*

FOOD & DRINK

BODEGÓN EL PUNTERO

A town restaurant in the style of country inn – choose from all the Canarian classics. The fish served here is especially good. *Closed Sun | C/ San Clemente 3 | tel. 9 22 28 22 14 | Budget*

IL GELATO DEL MERCATO

Tenerife's best ice cream can be found in the hustle-and-bustle of the market hall. *Tue–Sun 9:30am–3pm | C/ San Sebastián*

51 | Mercado de Nuestra Señora de África

INSIDER TIP ▶ LA HIERBITA

The "little herb" serves Canarian classics in the rustic atmosphere of a historic building in the Old Town. Do as the Spaniards do and order lots of tapas to share with one another! *Closed Sun | C/ Clavel 19 | tel. 9 22 24 46 17 | www.lahierbita.com | Budget–Moderate*

INSIDER TIP ▶ KIOSKO PRÍNCIPE

In a lovely garden right in the middle of town. This iron pavilion is a real gem – the choice of tapas is wide; the atmosphere under the tall trees cool and relaxed. *Daily | Plaza del Principe Asturias | tel. 9 22 24 74 40 | Budget*

LOS MENCEYES

Crystal chandeliers, upholstered chairs and elegant table presentations create a smart setting for international haute cuisine and new Canarian dishes. An army of waiters in tails stay calm and discreet even at busy times. One of the best restaurants on the island. *Daily | C/ Dr. Naveiras 38 | tel. 9 22 27 67 00 | Expensive*

SHOPPING

ARTENERIFE

On the Plaza de España stands a low, arcing pavilion covered in greenery belonging to the state art and craft chain. *Mon–Fri 10am–2pm and 5pm–8pm, Sat 10am–2pm | www.artenerife.com*

EL CORTE INGLÉS ●

This large department store in *Avenida Tres de Mayo* offers shoppers everything – from the latest fashions and DVDs to fine foods. On the top floor, the seventh, there is a ☙ panoramic restaurant (*Budget*).

MERCADO DE NUESTRA SEÑORA DE ÁFRICA

It is an exhilarating experience to take a tour of Santa Cruz's produce market, which occupies a beige, Moorish-style building. In the wide square and beneath the arcades of the two-storey building, traders offer animals, fruits, vegetables, fish, flowers, cheese and lots more *(daily 7am–3pm | C/ San Sebastián 51)*. On Sunday there's a flea market at the *mercado*.

ZARA

The now global Spanish fashion brand, renowned for affordable, but contemporary styles, has a branch in the pedestrian zone. *C/ del Castillo/Teobaldo Power*

ENTERTAINMENT

At the weekend, clubbers meet up on Av. De Anaga and in the La Noria area on the edge of the *barranco* (between the church and the bridge) – the party lasts until daybreak!

EL DESVÁN

Before and after party: crowds gather inside and outside to listen to jazz and live music, chill out and visit the art exhibitions. There are other popular evening haunts close by. *Daily from 5:30pm | Pasaje de Sitja 17 | www.eldesvan-santacruz.com*

INSIDER TIP LA NORIA

A new scene is emerging underneath the bridge. You can chill out in lounge style in *Bulan*. Beyond that they come thick and fast: in *Lagar* there's live music, opposite the cool *Mojos y Mojitos* and *Los Reunidos* bars, then comes the *Marqués de la Noria* bodega and the classic tasca *El Porrón*. *All daily from 8pm | C/ Antonio Domínguez Alfonso*

WHERE TO STAY

BARCELÓ SANTA CRUZ CONTEMPORANEO

The hotel's décor is modern and elegant, the rooms spacious and inviting. Sun loungers on the roof terrace. *150 rooms | Rambla de Santa Cruz 116 | tel. 9 71 21 19 01 | www.barcelo.com | Moderate*

MENCEY ●

This archetypal grand hotel in traditional Canarian architectural style is situated in the city centre, on the edge of the city park and beside the Rambla. The lobby and restaurant, lounges and bars evoke the spirit of a bygone age, but the rooms are thoroughly modern – unfussy and pure white. There is a palm garden with a pool and a large spa. *293 rooms | Av. Dr. José Naveiras 38 | tel. 9 22 60 99 00 | www.grandhotelmencey.com | Expensive*

TABURIENTE

This hotel by the Parque García Sanabria

is delightful. Sofa corners, period chests of drawers and crystal chandeliers create an atmosphere like staying with friends. Rooms in minimalist style. *116 rooms | Av. Dr. José Naveiras 24a | tel. 9 22 27 60 00 | www.hoteltaburiente.com | Budget–Moderate*

INFORMATION

OFICINA DE TURISMO
Plaza de España | tel. 9 22 23 95 92 | www.santacruzmas.com and www. elcorazondetenerife.com
The bright red ● *City Sightseeing Bus (Daily 10am–6pm | duration 75 min. | from 15.50 euros (online) | www.city-sightseeing.com)* picks up passengers right next to the tourist information centre.

WHERE TO GO

GRAN CANARIA (0) (*M 0*)
For a day trip to the neighbouring island to the east (for everything you need to know, see MARCO POLO Gran Canaria) take the Fred. Olsen Express catamaran from the harbour. This runs several times a day to Agaete and the crossing takes an hour *(return trip approx. 100 euros per person | tel. 9 02 10 01 07 | www.fredolsen.es).*

SAN ANDRÉS (139 E3) (*M O3*)
When the city fathers decided that Santa Cruz de Tenerife needed a beach, they looked closely at the fishing village of San Andrés 7 km (4 miles) to the northeast. But the volcanic-grey pebble beach at the foot of a steep gorge was not attractive enough, so in 1970 they brought in a few shiploads of fine Saharan sand from what was then the Spanish colony of Western Sahara. This was how the seaside resort of San Andrés came into being.
Gleaming brightly in golden yellow is the man-made kilometre-long beach ★ *Playa de las Teresitas*, now much enhanced by clusters of palm trees. To prevent the golden sands from being washed away, breakwaters were created. During the week it is

Sunbathing under palm trees, swimming protected by a breakwater: Playa de las Teresitas often very quiet. But on Saturday and Sunday, *Cruzeños* flock here in their thousands, but few tourists choose the most Canarian of all beaches.

There is a wide range of INSIDER TIP small restaurants serving seafood and fish in San Andrés. Two restaurants with good reputations are *El Rubi (daily | C/ El Dique 19 | Moderate)* and *Marisquería Ramón (daily | C/ El Dique 23 | Moderate)*, both with a large dining room and pond, from which fresh fish are caught for the table. Just want a snack? Then there's nothing nicer than hanging out in a *chiringuito*, one of the beach bars, shaded by palms with your feet in the sand.

TACORONTE

(137 E3) *(⌘ K3)* **As so often on Tenerife, the place is surrounded by bland new buildings; but on the other side of the main thoroughfare it has a pretty historical core.**

For wine connoisseurs, it is definitely worth a visit, because Tacoronte (pop.

22,000) lies at the heart of the largest wine growing area on the Canary Islands. Extensive vineyards extend along the fertile hillsides. The dozens of *bodegas,* and even more *guachinches,* i.e. improvised roadside taverns, can be very tempting and a good opportunity for a wine tasting.

SIGHTSEEING

EL CRISTO DE LOS DOLORES
This life-sized statue of Jesus dating from the 17th century stands in the church of a former Augustinian monastery. The triple-naved church also contains a wealth of silver work, including the altar and tabernacle in the chancel; the monastery has a beautiful cloister. *Daily | Plaza del Cristo*

WHERE TO GO

LA MATANZA DE ACENTEJO
(137 D–E4) *(⌘ J–K4)*
The place name meaning the "slaughter of Acentejo" recalls the momentous battle of 1494 between the Guanches and the Spanish conquerors. On that occasion the conquistadors suffered a humiliating defeat. Unfortunately, there's hardly anything historic in La Matanza; the faceless present prevails. An exception is the INSIDER TIP *La Cuadra de San Diego* estate *(closed Mon–Wed | Camino Botello 2 | TF-5, exit 23, then TF-217 | tel. 9 22 57 83 85 | www.lacuadradesandiego.es | Moderate)* dating back to the 16th century, a pretty restaurant with creative Canarian cuisine.

EL SAUZAL (137 E3–4) *(⌘ K3)*
Most visitors to Tacoronte's neighbouring town (pop. 8,000) head for the "house of wine", the INSIDER TIP *Casa del Vino (Tue 10:30am–6:30pm, Wed–Sat 9am–9pm | Sun 11am–6pm | admission 3 euros | www.casadelvinotenerife.com).*

Wine museum with a tasting room, tapas bar and restaurant: Casa del Vino

It is housed in an old 17th-century farm-house – with a lovely view of the sea and of Mount Teide. You'll see historic equipment including wooden wine presses, and much more, documenting the history of wine production on Tenerife. Glasses of the finest wines will be proffered to you in the cosy Tasca (2 euros per class).

The elegant Restaurante ☆ *Casa del Vino (closed Mon | tel. 9 22 56 38 86 | Moderate)* serves Canarian classics. You can ask to be seated on the terrace with sea view.

If you have a car, you can drive 1.5 km (1 mile) down to the town centre which "hangs" over the coastal cliffs on several terraces. Behind the ornate 16th-century Iglesia de *San Pedroaus*, you'll discover a romantic spot with a *museum (irregular opening hours)* to Tenerife's saint, María Sor Jesús. Another lovely spot is the ☆ *Mirador de Garañona* with its view of the surf thundering against the cliffs.

VALLE DE GUERRA (137 E–F2) *(⑰ K–L2)*
Wine is produced, fruit and vegetables grown and flowers cultivated in the Valle

de Guerra region north of Tacoronte. Just before you enter the town of the same name you will see on the left the *Museo de Antropología de Tenerife (Tue–Sun 9am–7pm | admission 3 euros | www. museosdetenerife.com)*. This anthropological museum, with exhibitions devoted to contemporary Canarian customs and traditions, occupies the grand *Casa de Carta*, an 18th-century farmhouse.

LA VICTORIA DE ACENTEJO
(137 D4–5) *(⑰ J4)*
That the Spanish eventually subjugated the natives is recalled 2 km (1.2 miles) further on in the name of La Matanza's neighbouring village. It means "the victory of Acentejo". Just over a year after the defeat the men returned, but this time with shining armour and an even larger army. The Guanches now had nothing with which to counter them and were finally defeated. To give thanks to God, Captain Fernandez de Lugo ordered his men to start work on a church, which was fittingly named *Nuestra Senora de las Victorias* and it stands to this day.

THE NATIONAL PARK

This is an absolute must-see! The ☼ **Parque Nacional del Teide** (141 E–F 4–6, 142 A–C 3–6) *(*∅ *E–H 6–8)* **lies at Alpine altitudes above 2,000 m (6,500 ft) and covers an area of over 135 km² (52 sq miles), making it the largest national park in the Canary Islands. At its heart lies a giant caldera by the name of Las Cañadas, shadowed by the almost 4,000 m (13,000 ft) high Mount Teide.**

You won't believe your eyes. The elliptical caldera of the Cañadas, with a diameter of 16 km (10 miles), is one of the world's largest craters, encircled by a 45 km (28 mile) long jagged rim. Here you'll experience a landscape in a state of upheaval: multi-coloured shimmering ash, broad plains and deep gorges. Screes are sometimes smooth and polished, sometimes

pock-marked. The "Mustard Mountain" *(Montaña Mostaza)* shines sulphur-yellow and the "White Mountain" *(Montaña Blanca)* bright white. The tongue-like slag fields are jet-black. Rocks, slammed into the earth, have jagged edges like black glass. Everywhere you go, you'll be surrounded by boulders that look as if they were strewn about by giants. And it's all outdone by striking peaks. The 3,000 m (10,000 ft) high volcanic chimney of the *Pico Viejo* towers on the northern edge of the two craters, where the last major eruption occurred in 1798. Recent studies suggest, however, that both the Cañadas and the La Orotava Valley were formed by landslides of almost unimaginable scale. 1,000 m³ (35,000 cubic feet) of earth fell into the sea during the forma-

Aloof and majestic – a visit to
Tenerife's National Park
is an impressive spectacle

tion of the Cañadas. It has been established that Mount Teide was formed almost
200,000 years ago, after the landslides,
and so in geological terms is still very
young. To compare, it was 7 million years ago that volcanic activity here raised
land from the floor of the Atlantic for the
first time, forming one of several islands
that would later fuse to make Tenerife.
You may feel in the national park like
you're on another planet due to the apparent lack of vegetation. This impression is deceptive, however, as 139 species

have adjusted to the extreme climatic
conditions at high altitude. They have to
contend with strong sunshine during the
day, freezing temperatures at night and
drought. A good 20 per cent of plants
are endemic to Tenerife, i.e. they don't
exist anywhere else in the world. These
include the pillared *tajinaste rojo* with its
bright red flowers (Mount Teide bugloss),
the little yellow or white Teide daisy and
the Teide violet. Plants at this altitude
stay in flower for only a short period, just
May and June. Few vertebrates survive

in these harsh conditions, with mouflon sheep returned to the wild, finches and kestrels being among the exceptions.

You can break your tour through the *Parque Nacional* in two places: the ● ☀ *Roques de García* (142 A6) (*☐ F8*), also called simply *Los Roques*, is an ensemble of multi-coloured rock outcrops. A viewing platform offers a spectacular view. If you climb a little higher, you will be rewarded with a stunning vista down into the *Llano de Ucanca*, the largest plain in the Teide-Cañadas and also of *Los Azulejos,* a shimmering rock formation in a greenish blue, due to the high iron hydrate content.

The second stop is the ☀ *Pico del Teide* (142 A4) (*☐ F7*) itself. Its almost symmetrical summit cone reaches a height of 3,718 m (12,198 ft). Its name is derived from the Guanche word for hell. Emerging from its flanks come hot (up to 86°C) sulphurous vapours, proof that hell still stirs. The ★ *Teleférico (daily 9am–4pm in good weather, in May usually closed for maintenance | round trip 26 euros | www.teleferico-teide.com),* the Mount Teide cable car, climbs 1,200 m (3,940 ft) to La Rambleta mountain station at 3,550 m (11,647 ft) in 10 minutes. From there you can take walks to ☀ *La Fortaleza* lookout point and the ☀ *Pico Viejo* (3,135 m/10,285 ft) – but be warned: a strong wind often blows! Before or after your ride to the summit, you can sample the refreshments served in the panoramic cafeteria at the valley station.

Only guests at the *Refugio Altavista*, the hostel at the foot of the mountain, can climb to the top of the volcano without a permit between 5pm and 9am the following day – otherwise you must obtain a special permit from the *Centro de Visitantes Telesforo Bravo del Parque* (see p. 42) in La Orotava. There, or online at *www.reservasparquesnacionales.es*, you can also book an overnight stay at the *Refugio*.

(see p. 42)

WHERE TO STAY

PARADOR NACIONAL ☀
(142 A5) (*☐ F8*)

The chalet-style hotel belonging to the state-run chain is the highest hotel in the Canaries. Excellent Canarian cuisine served at the on-site restaurant *(Expensive)*, rustic-style setting, pool. *37 rooms | Las Cañadas del Teide | tel. 9 22 38 64 15 | www.parador.es | Moderate*

LOW BUDGET

The *El Portillo visitors' centre (see p. 71)* provides free information sheets for two to five-hour hikes through the national park. Ask in advance if there are any guided hiking tours organised!

Mount Teide Observatory organises free tours for individuals and groups, but by prior appointment only.

(see p. 71)

HIKES

Marked ★ ☀ *walking paths* lead through the Cañadas and up to Mount Teide. When climbing Spain's highest mountain, you'll pass by the "Teide Eggs", *Huevos del Teide*, huge boulders of lava rock scattered about the area. Please be aware, however, that high altitude puts the body under severe strain. Before undertaking longer walks, make sure you are fully acclimatised. Sun protection and plenty of water are essential for all hikes in the national park.

CENTRO DE VISITANTES CAÑADA BLANCA (142 A5) *(🕮 G8)*

As soon as renovations are finished, a visitor centre will open next to the *parador*, where pictures, wall charts and multimedia displays provide background information on the National Park. *Daily 9am–4pm | admission free*

CENTRO DE VISITANTES EL PORTILLO
● (142 B4) *(🕮 G6)*

A visitor centre in a simulated lava tunnel with display panels, a multimedia interpretation of the National Park and a botanical garden where you can investigate Teide flora. *Daily 9am–4pm | admission free | at El Portillo at the north-eastern exit of the Cañadas | tel. 9 22 35 60 00*

WHERE TO GO

OBSERVATORIO DEL TEIDE ●
(142 C4) *(🕮 H7–8)*

The strange white towers at the eastern entrance to Teide National Park belong to the Tenerife Observatory. When the Canarian Institute of Astrophysics started its work on this site in 1964, it seemed that here – well away from civilisation and at an altitude of 2,390 m (7,841 ft) – was the ideal place to view the heavens.

But today the lights from the holiday resorts interfere with the work of the astronomers, so they now observe the night sky from the neighbouring island of La Palma and scientists at the Observatory study the sun during the day. The scientists at Tenerfie Observatory study the sun during the day. If you would like a tour (only Apr–Dec), you must register, ideally by completing the form on their website: *tel. 9 22 65 62 62 | www.iac.es/ot/visitas.*

A journey through the National Park is the highlight of a visit to Tenerife

★ **Teleférico**
Spectacular – the cable-car ride to Spain's highest mountain → **p. 70**

★ **Hikes**
Incredible – nature amidst fields of lava in the Cañadas→ **p. 70**

MARCO POLO HIGHLIGHTS

THE SOUTHEAST

There are few hidden charms in this region. Arid and sun-bleached land, spoilt plains and a few sleepy towns. And it can get very dusty – and gusty – with peripheral trade winds casting a milky veil over the sun.

The central altitudes with their terraced fields are a prettier sight. They are propped up with nearly infinite strings of pumice stone walls criss-crossing the landscape. Fruits and vegetables are grown here, and lots of wine. The pastures are home to goats and sheep whose milk is used to make good cheese. If you have the time, it's worth taking the drive along the old, winding TF-28 highway from Los Cristianos to Santa Cruz de Tenerife. Not only are there many fine views en route, but the road is also lined by villages inhabited by people whose lifestyle has changed little since the arrival of mass tourism.

CANDELARIA

(143 F2–3) (*M L5–6*) **In this small town of 20,000 inhabitants, everything relates to the Virgen de Candelaria, Tenerife's patron saint.**

A huge pilgrimage is celebrated in her honour every August, and even at other times of the year, the stream of pilgrims never lets up. It is pleasant to take a stroll through the Old Town with its traffic-calmed,, sometimes rather steep, lanes and small shops and the broad square that opens up towards the ocean

At home with the locals – the southeast of Tenerife has so far remained largely untouched by tourism

SIGHTSEEING

BASÍLICA DE CANDELARIA

The triple-naved basilica built in 1959 in a rather fanciful Canarian/neo-colonial style is home to the archipelago's most revered shrine, the ★ *Virgen de Candelaria*. The extravagantly clad Virgin adorned with crown and jewels occupies a place of honour in a gold-framed, illuminated chamber above the altar. A modern mural tells the story behind the statue. Lost during a storm in 1826, a

replacement was made in 1827 by the *Tinerfeño* artist, Fernando Estévez.

PLAZA DE LA PATRONA DE CANARIAS

The vast square in front of the cathedral was built for the throngs of pilgrims, who come every year in mid-August to pay homage to the Virgen de Candelaria. Highly visible on the waterfront are nine rather strange, larger-than-life *bronze statues*. They were created in 1993 by the Canarian artist, José Abad, and represent the *menceys*, who ruled over Tenerife at the time of the Spanish conquest. The Guanche kings are dressed in animal skins and bear spears, sticks and mallets. With their clean-cut faces, athletic bodies and flowing hair, they embody the ideal of the noble savage. On the square, the traditional, terraced restaurant *Plaza (daily | tel. 9 22 50 42 31*

de Canarias. At the weekend you will find crafts, knick-knacks and devotional objects on sale, on Wednesday farmers from the surrounding area come into Candelaria to sell their wares, mainly ✪ fruit, vegetables, cheese and wine. *Sat, Sun 9am–2pm crafts, Wed 5pm–9pm farmers' market.*

This faithful replica of Thor Heyerdahl's Ra II can be seen near the Pirámides de Güímar

| Moderate) serves good, down-to-earth Canarian food. After refreshment, you might feel like an exploratory tour of the town, but that could involve a steep climb. The small bell tower, which rises above the jumble of houses, is part of the Baroque *Iglesia de Santa Ana* (1575).

SHOPPING

MERCADILLO

Three times a week a small market is held at the entrance to the pedestrian-only road, which leads to the Plaza Patrona

GÜIMAR

(143 E3–4) (🜨 K6) Many people have heard of the Pyramids of Güímar, but few know of the town itself. It lies in the Valle de Güímar, which was formed 800,000 years ago in a landslide caused by a violent earthquake.

Once an agricultural centre, nowadays wine – which is more profitable – is produced all around Güímar (pop. 19,000). The bright green foliage of the vines stands out on the terraced fields.

Güímar's small Old Town with its church and stately homes are left over from days of bygone wealth. The "Pyramids" date back to the time when Güímar was the capital of a *menceyato*, a Guanche kingdom. Its last ruler submitted to the Spanish conquerors and assisted them in their conquest of the island's eight remaining kingdoms.

SIGHTSEEING

IGLESIA SAN PEDRO APÓSTOL

The church, built in 1610, boasts wooden ceilings, a carved pulpit and the circular retables (altarpieces). The illusionistic painting behind the altar, which appears to lengthen the nave, is also noteworthy. *Plaza San Pedro*

PIRÁMIDES DE GÜÍMAR ★ ●

Spread over a large expanse of land to the north of the town are six stone pyramids. In earlier times, farmers dried their fruit and vegetables on the steps and gave no thought to their origins or strange architecture. Why should they? The whole eastern part of the island was criss-crossed by stone walls and every generation added new ones. It needed an outsider to take a closer look at these piles of rocks. Having studied the alignment of the pyramids and carried out a survey of their exact location, the Norwegian ethnographer Thor Heyerdahl concluded that they were probably used for sacred rituals and that they have astronomical orientations. He also believed they formed a transatlantic link between the ancient Egyptian pyramids and those of the Maya in America.

An *ethnographic park (daily 9:30am –6pm | admission 11 euros | C/ Chacona | www.piramidesdeguimar.es)* vividly illustrates these theories and also sheds new light on the culture of the aboriginal inhabitants. In the park is a replica of "Ra II", the 12-m (40-ft) long ship Heyerdahl made from reeds. In 1970 he successfully crossed the Atlantic on the original vessel.

FOOD & DRINK
WHERE TO STAY

CASONA SANTO DOMINGO

This town house dates from the 16th century. Six small, charming rooms, bodega and good restaurant. *C/ Santo Domingo 32 | tel. 9 22 51 02 29 | www.casonasanto domingo.com | Moderate*

CASAS ITER ⊙ (147 D4) (ⵯ H–J11)

In the shadow of whirring wind turbines – connected to a technology park 35 km (22 miles) south of Güímar – are 24 futuristic *casas bioclimáticas*, designed by architects from around the world that want to realise here their vision of a house that is powered by wind and

---

★ Virgen de Candelaria
The Canary Islands' most revered shrine: the dark-skinned madonna → p. 73

★ Pirámides de Güímar
Mysterious stone pyramids and a reed ship → p. 75

★ Vilaflor
Famed for its spring water and as Spain's highest municipality → p. 76

★ Paisaje lunar
A "lunar landscape" of bizarre volcanic tuff → p. 77

MARCO POLO HIGHLIGHTS

solar energy and gets its water from its very own seawater desalination plant. The houses couldn't be any more different: sun-collecting glass cubes contrast with bunkers sunk into the ground and playful round buildings with severe rectangles. To stay there, you'll need a rental car and earplugs. *24 houses | Polígono Industrial de Granadilla | Granadilla de Abona | tel. 9 22 74 77 00 | casas.iter.es | Moderate–Expensive*

HOTEL RURAL FINCA SALAMANCA

In the centre of an avocado *finca* in 5-ha (12-acre) grounds lies the historic manor house with 20 country-style rooms and pretty salons. Guests can dine within the old walls of the restaurant (*Budget*) on Spanish and Canarian dishes. There is also a ✶ magnificent garden with a pool and a view of Mount Teide. *Directions: Ctra. Güímar–El Puertito, km 1.5 | tel. 9 22 51 45 30 | www.hotel-fincasalamanca.com | Moderate*

LOW BUDGET

For just 36 euros a night (minimum stay three nights), you can stay at the secluded house *La Hoyita (1 room | www.casalahoyita.com)* near Güímar.

In Europe's largest moringa garden, you can find out everything there is to know about this "miracle plant" for free if you book in advance: *Moringa Garden (Mon–Sat 10am–6pm | Camino Chinguaro 1 | tel. 9 22 51 50 74 | www.moringagarden.eu)*

WHERE TO GO

ARAFO (143 E3) (*⌘ K6*)

A gem in this village (pop. 5,000) 4 km (2.5 miles) north of Güímar is the laurel-shaded plaza with a small bar (*Daily | Budget*).

ARICO (147 D–E2) (*⌘ J9*)

This small town (pop. 7,000), comprising several districts spread out along the main road, lies 29 km (18 miles) south of Güímar. *Arico Nuevo* is protected, because of its status as a Site of Special Historical Architectural Interest. Lining both sides of the downhill by-road off the main highway are some beautifully preserved village houses and a quiet plaza with chapel, all neatly white-washed and with doors and window frames in classic Canarian green – something of a rarity for Tenerife. **INSIDER TIP** Typical Canarian accommodation is available in the ✶ *Casa La Verita* and the ✶ *Casa Cha Carmen*, two country houses in the hills between Arico and Fasnia. Traditional architecture combines with modern comforts; the magnificent vista, barbecue area and vegetable garden are a bonus (*tel. 9 22 50 07 09 | www.lasombrera.com | Moderate*).

PORÍS DE ABONA (147 F2) (*⌘ K9*)

Around 2,000 people live in this fishing village located 18 km (11 miles) south of Güímar and boasts a winding harbour promenade, plus a beach right next to it, if you need to cool down. The ✶ *Café al Mar (daily | mobile tel. 6 36 94 38 20 | Budget)*, is worth the detour for the view of the bay and the delicious tapas.

VILAFLOR ★ (146 B3) (*⌘ F9*)

If you drive into the national park from the south, you'll pass through this somwehat sleepy town of 3,000. Vilaflor is among the highest municipalities in

Spain. Around the town, which stands at 1,400 m (4,600 ft) above sea level, are many hectares of terraced fields, where local farmers grow vines and vegetables. One small business bottles spring water under the brand names of "Pinalito" and "Fuente Alta" which is drunk everywhere on Tenerife. There is also an outlet for what is now a rare craft – just like their great-grandmothers some of the women in the village still make *rosetas*, filigree ● lace rosettes, which are sewn on to blankets and shawls. You can find the lace on sale in the souvenir shops on the church square, where the women will happily demonstrate the extremely time-consuming art of lace-making.

Daily life in Vilaflor is undemanding. Far away from the bustle of the holiday centres and the dusty coastline, here you can breathe in the fresh mountain air of the Mount Teide region. The single-nave *Iglesia de San Pedro Apóstol* from the mid-16th century dominates the town's central square. The impressive *Casa de los Soler* façade on the back of the chapel is testimony to the former power held by the noble family who founded the town.. At the cosy *Hotel Rural el Sombrerito (20 rooms | C/ Santa Catalina 15 | tel. 9 22 70 90 52 | Budget)*, a simple country inn, a holiday away from all bustle becomes a reality. Another gem is the four-star **INSIDERTIP** Spa Villalba *(22 rooms | Ctra. San Roque 4 | tel. 9 22 70 99 30 | www. hotelvillalba.com | Moderate)*, with pine garden, sun terrace, spa, gym and pool. It is popular with hikers, bikers and climbers. In the town centre, you can have a good meal in cosy surroundings at the **INSIDERTIP** Rincón del Roberto *(closed Tue | Av. Hermano Pedro 27 | tel. 9 22 70 90 35 | Moderate)* , where Señora Araceli and her husband Jesús serve up Canarian classics (tasty: rabbit and goat meat!) and dry local wines.

Tenerife's lunar landscape: Paisaje Lunar

Starting just above Vilaflor are forests of Canary Island pines. One famous example of the species, the ● *Pino Gordo*, reaches a height of 60 m (almost 200 ft). It's by the TF-21 road that winds its way up to Mount Teide, passing some ☼ stunning viewpoints at the very top of Tenerife on its way. One curiosity is the ★ *Paisaje lunar* (146 B2) *(∅ G8)*, the "lunar landscape", a bizarre volcanic formation unique to the Canaries. It is to be found 20 km (12 miles) to the northeast of Vilaflor (turn right near the km 65 marker, hiking time 2.5 hrs/9 km (6 miles) each way).

THE SOUTHWEST

Some 3.5 million of the 4.9 million visitors who come to Tenerife every year make for the southwest. This is where the finest beaches are and where sunshine is practically guaranteed. Over the last decades, an infrastructure that perfectly meets the needs of mass tourism has emerged – hotels ranging from affordable to super luxury, shopping centres, restaurants to suit all tastes, entertainment around the clock, plus leisure activities from sailing to scuba diving.

It is also the location for the largest and finest water park on the Canaries – Siam Park. There are also half a dozen golf courses, plus a number of marinas, from where pleasure boats leave for tours. The global financial crisis has brought the building boom to an end until further notice. The golf courses with their grandiose club houses, a huge convention centre, expressways and mega-hotels built on what was formerly barren wasteland prove how easy it once was to attract investment.

But this dramatic transformation has endangered the traditional lifestyle of the locals. Agriculture is now is of little importance; the fields lie fallow. There are some vast banana plantations between Guía de Isora and Puerto de Santiago and in the hinterland of the Costa del Silencio. In the south, tourism has brought prosperity. The holiday centres are now providing work for many villagers – it's not a change that everyone welcomes, but in this arid region there are few alternatives.

If you want beach, sunshine and action 24/7, the island's south coast is the place to be

LOS CRISTIANOS

MAP ON PAGE 86
(144–145 C–D5) (*M E11*) Los Cristianos, the oldest resort in the south isn't particularly beautiful at first sight: joyless sleeping quarters, traffic chaos, hardly any trees. The local council has pulled the emergency brakes and started to give the place a facelift. Roads have been traffic-calmed and lined with palms and the promenades smartened up, much to the delight of the many holidaymakers that swear by Los Cristianos because it still has local life.

The beach promanade links the new and old parts of the town. At the front of the bay, the beach teems with swimmers, further out fishing boats and ferries ply in and out. Strollers almost unwittingly seem to end up in the small part of the town above the harbour, which with its narrow alleys and tiny courtyards serves

Rows on rows of hotels with a mountain backdrop: Los Cristianos

as a reminder that the now bustling seaside resort was once a quiet village.

FOOD & DRINK

INSIDER TIP CASA TAGORO

The best restaurant far and wide: enjoy a special evening in this restaurant decorated with antique furniture and half-open kitchen where the German chef Gerhard Brodträger dreams up his culinary creations inspired by both the Mediterranean region and his alpine heritage. It serves a wide variety of tapas and the degustation menus are highly recommended! The eatery is slightly hidden behind the Reverón Plaza hotel. *Tue–Sat 6pm–11pm, Sun 1pm–12pm | C/ Valle de Menéndez 28 | tel. 8 22 66 08 33 | www. casatagoro.com | Moderate-Expensive*

EL CINE

One of the town's oldest restaurants tucked away in a small alleyway close to the promenade offering simple and authentic food just like it has always done. There is a limited yet always freshly made choice of dishes. That said, the traditional wrinkly potatoes *(papas arrugadas)* with mojo sauce are always on the menu. *Closed Mon | C/ Juan Bariajo 8 | mobile tel. 6 09 10 77 58 | Budget–Moderate*

MESÓN CASTELLANO

In a rustic Castilian setting surrounded by hunting trophies, lots of wood and wrought-iron chandeliers, Señor Manuel José serves excellent meat dishes, grills included, plus wine from the mainland. *Closed Tue | C/ Alfonso Domínguez 40 | El Camisón | tel. 9 22 79 63 09 | www.mesoncastellano.com | Moderate*

PICCOLO PALADAR

As the Italian name suggests, it's all about antipasti, pasta Roman style and changing specials every day – on a terrace overlooking the sea above Playa de las Vistas. *Closed Tue | Av. Habana 11 | tel. 9 22 79 67 88 | Moderate*

SHOPPING

LA ALPIZPA
Canarian crafts produced by people with disabilities are on sale in this stall on the *Playa de los Cristianos* promenade. *Mon–Sat 10am–1pm and 5pm–8:30pm*

INSIDER TIP ▶ LIBRERÍA BARBARA
Bookshop with Spanish, English, German and French titles, plus maps and guidebooks. *Mon–Fri 10am–1pm and 5pm–7:30pm, Sat 10am–1pm | C/ Juan Pablo Abril 6*

MERCADILLO
At the popular Sunday flea market *(rastro)* between Arona Gran Hotel and the beach, you'll find much commerce and kitsch, but also beautiful craftwork sometimes. *Sun 9am–2pm*

BEACHES

PLAYA DE LOS CRISTIANOS
The 1 km (0.6 miles) long and up to 100 m (330 ft) wide beach starts right next to the fishing and ferry harbour and has its own lifeguard station. But the water might not necessarily be clean.

PLAYA DE LAS VISTAS
The beach connecting Los Cristianos with Playa de las Américas has been laid out with fine, golden sand It is 1.5 km (1 mile) long and protected by breakwaters, so ideal for swimming. At this point the swell is slightly higher, the wind a little stronger.

SPORTS & LEISURE

Here in the south there is hardly a sport you can't pursue: squash, golf and mini-golf, trampolining, parachute jumping, hang-gliding, hiking, cycling, climbing, sailing, windsurfing, jet skiing, scuba diving, deep sea fishing and much more. To find out what exactly is on offer, take a walk along the beach, around the harbours and in the shopping malls – you will see for yourself what the various options are. Or go to one of the tourist offices and pick up a brochure.

BOAT EXCURSIONS
Excursion ships set sail from the harbour every day when the sea is calm – from pirate windjammers to whale-watching and deep-sea fishing boats. *Information and tickets are available at the end of the promenade just before the harbour*

CAMEL PARK
Dromedary rides, taking 50 minutes, start from *La Camella*, which is situated inland a short distance from Los Cristianos. *Daily 10am–5pm | rides 20 euros per person | location: TF-51 3.5 km (2 miles) | free*

★ **El Médano**
A mecca for windsurfing and a meeting place for young holidaymakers → p. 84

★ **Los Gigantes**
Towering up behind the village – truly gigantic cliffs → p. 95

★ **Playa de la Arena**
An extraordinary sight – a beach with jet-black sand → p. 94

★ **Barranco del Infierno**
Hike through a natural oasis in the hinterland of the south coast → p. 91

MARCO POLO HIGHLIGHTS

shuttle bus from the south coast | tel. 9 22 72 11 21 | www.camelpark.es

GOLF

There are five golf-courses in the surrounding area. The green fee for 18 holes is between approx. 60 euros in the summer and about double that in the winter. The *Amarilla Golf & Country Club (direc-*

In the evening Los Cristianos quickly quietens down. There is some nightlife along the promenade, the *Paseo Marítimo*. It's a little bit livelier along *Av. de Suecia*. There are a series of cocktail bars, including the *Agua de Coco*. And in the *San Telmo* shopping centre behind the Playa

A wonderful place to learn golf! Golf del Sur offers a golf school.

tions: Autopista del Sur, Los Abrigos exit, 3 km/2 miles | tel. 9 22 73 03 19 | www. amarillagolf.es) has 18 holes, a 9-hole pitch and putt course, plus riding stables, tennis courts and swimming pools. *Golf del Sur (directions: Autopista del Sur, Los Abrigos exit, 4 km/2.5 miles | tel. 9 22 73 81 70 | www.golfdelsur.es)* is a 27-hole golf course, plus golf academy.

Golf Center Los Palos *(directions: Autopista del Sur, Guaza exit, km 1.5 | tel. 9 22 16 90 80 | www.golflospalos.com)* is an attractive 9-hole course offering golf classes for both beginners and advanced players.

de las Vistas, there are a few pubs.

INSIDER TIP ▶ MAR Y SOL

This spa hotel offers wheelchair-accessible apartments fitted with natural, non-allergenic materials. The restaurant serves vegetarian meals and will prepare food for guests with special dietary requirements. Treatments available in the therapy and rehabilitation centre range from massages and acupuncture to a rose oil bath. Fine views out to sea. The pools (one with water at 32° C) have access aids and hydro massages – and there's always a lifeguard on duty. Free beach shuttle bus, emergency service, diving school for the disabled, sports hall, golf courses and lots more. *234 apartments | Av. Amsterdam 8 | tel. 9 22 75 05 40 | www.marysol.org | Moderate*

PARADISE PARK FUN LIFESTYLE
This all-inclusive aparthotel is perfect for everyone: those looking for action, and those who just want a break. Entertainment with lots of sport, but also oases of calm. Guests praise the rooms, the food and the service. *280 rooms, 110 apartments | Urbanización Oasis del Sur | tel. 9 22 75 72 27 | www.hotelparadisepark. com | Moderate*

REVERÓN PLAZA
The four-star hotel is centrally located opposite the church and only a few metres from the beach. If you need peace and quiet, ask for a room on the fourth or fifth floor. Attractive ⚓ breakfast restaurant with harbour view, rooftop terrace with pool. *43 rooms | tel. 9 22 75 71 20 | www.labrandareveronplaza.com | Budget–Moderate*

INFORMATION

OFICINA DE TURISMO
Paseo Marítimo Playa de las Vistas | tel. 9 22 78 70 11 | www.arona.travel

WHERE TO GO

LOS ABRIGOS (146 C5) (*ØØ G12*)
The abiding image of the village (pop. 2,000) is one of the unusual angular-shaped residential blocks made of grey cement. It is situated 15 km (9 miles) east of Los Cristianos. Only after you go directly to the harbour area will you discover why tourists from all over the south flock

here every day. Lining the promenade are several restaurants. Most of them have beautiful sea views and are small and fairly basic, but they serve simply prepared, excellent dishes of fish and shellfish, which go pretty well straight from fishing boat into sauté pan. The best sea view is from the ⚓ narrow terrace of the *Perlas del Mar (closed Mon | tel. 9 22 17 00 14 | Moderate)*, the last restaurant on the cape. Watch the boats sailing in and out while enjoying a plate of fresh fish, potatoes and mojo sauce. A small market is held every Tuesday from 6pm to 9pm.

COSTA DEL SILENCIO
(145 D–E6) (*ØØ F12*)
Coast of Silence – this is not the most fitting name for the most southern point of

LOW BUDGET

The cost of amusement parks, discos, the casino, etc. can quickly mount up in Los Cristianos and Playa de las Américas. But promotional leaflets that grant free admission or discounts are distributed in hotels and out on the streets.

Folk events are held for tourists during the winter months. Once a week folklore musicians and dancers make their way along the promenade – in Los Cristianos, Playa de las Américas and Las Galletas.

The delicious and sumptuous three-course set menus in the *La Fortuna Nova* restaurant *(closed Sun | Av. del Valle Menéndez | | tel. 9 22 79 51 92)* in Los Cristianos are available at lunch for as low as just under 10 euros.

Tenerife, 12 km (7 miles) southeast of Los Cristianos. Planes land at the nearby airport almost every minute during the high season. And the landscape behind the town isn't particularly stunning; banana plantations behind high walls and expanses of plastic sheeting protecting the fields of vegetable don't exactly make for a romantic atmosphere.

The former fishing port of *Las Galletas* still has a small promenade with fish restaurants, such as the basic *Marina (daily | Budget–Moderate)* and the smarter *Atlántida (daily | Budget–Moderate)*.

LA GOMERA (0) (*✿ 0*)

Several times a day the *Fred. Olsen Express hydrofoil (return passage from 68 euros per person | tel. 9 02 10 01 07 | www.fredolsen.es)* whisks passengers from Los Cristianos harbour across to the neighbouring island of La Gomera (journey time approx. 40 minutes). It's an interesting destination for a day trip. A slightly cheaper alternative is the slightly slower ferry operated by the *Naviera Armas* shipping company *(tel. 9 02 45 65 00 | www.navieraarmas.es)*.

EL MÉDANO ★ (147 D5) (*✿ H11*)

El Médano ("The Dune"), located 20 km (12 miles) east of Los Cristianos, has Tenerife's longest natural beaches. Just over 2 km in length, the *Playa Médano*, which starts in the heart of the resort, boasts fine, golden sand. Swimmers frolic near the shore – but you have to be careful, because wind and kite surfers, who should theoretically be ploughing through the water much farther away, often stray towards the beach. They like El Médano for its prevailing strong winds, which may spoil a day at the beach for "normal" holidaymakers ...

A volcanic rock, the *Montaña Roja*, towers above the beach. Behind the "Red Mountain" towards Los Abrigos lies the

You have to just eat fish here – all along the coast, there are restaurants right next to the sea

coarse-sand beach of *Playa de la Tejita;* it's 1 km (0.6 miles) in length and always very windy. Nudists have claimed the first part of it for themselves.

El Médano (pop. 3,000) is still a rather sleepy spot – partly thanks to the surfers. There are still more locals than tourists. On the broad *Plaza Príncipe de Asturias* young northern Europeans and Canarians take a break over a beer. A kiosk provides everyone with information *(tel. 9 22 17 60 02)*. In the *Caballo Blanco (closed Fri | Paseo El Picacho 8 | Moderate)* you can have fish while sitting on the sun terrace above the surf.

The village can boast of plenty of good places to stay: located near the family-run hotel, *Playa Sur Tenerife (74 rooms | tel. 9 22 17 61 20 | www. hotelplayasurtenerife.com | Moderate)*, is the *Surf Center (tel. 22 17 91 77 | www. surfcenter.eu)*, which hires out boards (77 euros/day, 270 euros per week) and gives tuition to advanced surfers (from 40 euros). Hotel *Médano (91 rooms | tel. 9 22 17 70 00 | www.medano.es | Moderate)*, elderly, but now refreshed, is situated by the beach in the centre of the town and is very popular with young people.

North of El Médano lie the stony *Playa del Cabezo* and *Playa de la Jaquita* – both are surfing beaches used regularly as venues for international competitions.

PLAYA DE LAS AMÉRICAS

★ MAP ON PAGE 86

(144 C4–5) (ⵥ E11) **Seamlessly merging with Los Cristianos to the north is the tourist stronghold of Playa de las Américas, which further north becomes the more elegant Costa Adeje and Bahía del Duque resorts. A roundel of good beaches protected by breakwaters and with all the trimmings is a great place for holidaymakers to feel comfortable.**

A car-free, palm-lined beach promenade stretches down the full length of the resort towns, with loose rows of restaurants and shops.

Behind it are hotels, apartment complexes, shopping malls with outdoor excursion agencies and restaurants where you can feel right at home with English, Scandinavian or German cuisine. But don't worry: there are a couple of Spanish restaurants too. While Playa de las Américas has seen better days, the Costa Adeje and even more so, Bahía del Duque, are calmer and nicer-looking. The elegant hotels there court a wealthy clientele, but their beaches are open to the public.

FOOD & DRINK

LA CASITA DE TABY

This little tapas bar is hidden away an unaesthetic shopping mall shopping mall. The committed owners serve up a wide selection of Spanish home cooking – from potato salad to cheese and sausage platters and squid. Atmospheric in the evening with the artfully lit promenade. *Daily | Av. Puig Lluvina | C.C. Salytien | mobile tel. 65 19 88 75 | Budget*

FRIENDS LOUNGE BAR

The name says it all: casual, informal atmosphere along the beach promenade, friendly service and simple dishes. You're welcome to stop by even if it's just for a drink. *Daily | Paseo Tarajal | C.C. Compostela Beach | tel. 9 22 78 94 66 | www.friendstenerife.com | Budget– Moderate*

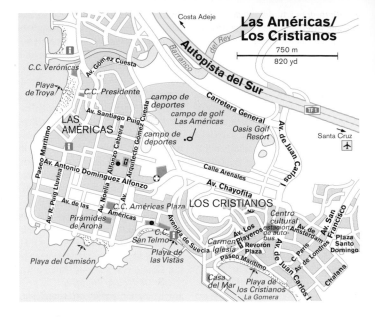

INSIDER TIP ► EL GOMERO

The Canarian answer to pizza and burger bars. A very simple, rustic restaurant serving a wide range of good Spanish-Canarian dishes – all at very affordable prices. Very popular and often busy. Affordable lunch menu. *Closed Sun | Av. V Centenario 1 | tel. 9 22 75 07 13 | Budget–Moderate*

PAPAGAYO BEACH CLUB

Excellent location on the promenade under palm trees with sounds of the waves crashing in the background. Glistening white interior design with a wide choice of cocktails and small snacks served all day long. DJ sessions and live flamenco organised in the evenings several times a week. *Daily 10am–3am, at weekends until 6am | Paseo Marítimo/ Av. Rafael Puig Lluvina | on the border with Costa Adeje | tel. 9 22 78 89 16 | www.papagayobeachclub.com | Budget*

SUGAR & SPICES

This fashionable, black and white themed restaurant serves mainly Italian classics. Popular choices include pappardelle with cep mushrooms, tortellini with spinach and "Diana" perch, garnished with mussels and prawns. *Daily | Av. Rafael Puig Llavina | Village Club | tel. 9 22 79 22 71 | Moderate*

SHOPPING

There are plenty of malls *(centros comerciales)* with outlets selling everything from kitschy souvenirs to high-value jewellery.

ARTENERIFE

The state-run handicrafts chain's stall at Playa de Troya looks like the sawn off hull of a ship. You're guaranteed to find Canarian products here – each item is unique. *Mon–Fri 10am–8:30pm,*

Sat 10am–1pm | Av. del Litoral. There is another Artenerife shop at the western end of Playa de las Vistas.

SIAM MALL

A free bus will take you to the beautiful, exotically styled shopping mall next to Siam Park. The selection of shops isn't just limited to brand names (Mango, Zara etc.); you'll also find nice local retailers. Park your kids in the playground and your car in the free car park. *Daily 9:30am–6:30pm | Av. Siam 3 | free shuttle from several hotels every 30 min. | ccsiammall.com*

BEACHES

Below the promenade, many small beaches have been created, all with fine, golden sand and protected from the surf by breakwaters. So they are perfectly safe for children. From *Playa de Troya* in the south to *Playa La Pinta* beyond Puerto Colón, the beaches lie in close succession. The beaches further north are quieter and there's more space.

PLAYA DEL CAMISÓN

At the very southern tip and with a view over Los Cristianos is this gem of a beach – some 500 m (1,640 ft) of golden sand below the promenade and the Mare Nostrum resort at the base of a palm-lined slope, with no traffic to negotiate and plenty of cafés and cool beach bars to supply the sun worshippers with food and drink. Walk a bit further along the coastal promenade and you will come to a much-favoured spot – for a memorable sunset, sit and enjoy a sundowner in the ⚘ ● *Chiringuito Bar (daily | Budget–Moderate)* of the *Villa Cortés* hotel, plus great view across to La Gomera.

Dazzling blue sea, fine sand, palm trees and sun loungers: Playa del Duque

PLAYA DEL DUQUE

The northernmost is also the finest beach. No wonder it's called "the duke's beach". 600 m (2,000 ft) of light sand with blue and white pavilions for changing cabins, overlooked by some majestic grand hotels.

PLAYA DE FAÑABÉ

Some 800 m (2,624 ft) in length and in a quiet spot, it's perfect for a relaxing after-

71 45 00 | www.bonadea2catamaran.com) cost from 25 euros, 49 euros for an excursion on the double-masted *Shogun (tel. 22 79 80 44 9)*. *Royal Delfin (from 45 euros | tel. 9 22 75 00 85 | www.tenerifedolphin. com)* organises daily boat tours to Los Gigantes and Masca.

Safari BOB Diving (55 euros | mobile tel. 6 70 83 95 16 | www.bob-diving.com) offers a variation on traditional scuba diving. Underwater scooters can be used by anyone.

Tenerife from the water: a nostalgic boat tour on a brig at Las Américas

noon sunbathing and swimming.

SPORTS & LEISURE

Like in the neighbouring town of Los Cristianos, there's a wide range of outdoor activities.

BOAT TRIPS AND DIVING EXCURSIONS

All the companies that offer these activities are located in *Puerto Colón* harbour. Two-hour catamaran trips with or without food on board on the *Bonadea (tel. 9 22*

GOLF

The 18-hole Golf Las Américas course *(directions: TF-1, exit 28 | tel. 9 22 75 20 05 | www.golf-tenerife.com)* is located on 90 ha (225 acres) of land near the resort. Green fee: 59–102 euros depending on the season, online booking possible.

The 27-hole *Costa Adeje Golf (Finca de los Olivos | directions: TF-1 to Guía de Isora, exit to La Caleta | tel. 9 22 71 00 00 | www. golfcostaadeje.com)* blends perfectly with the environment. Green fee: An 18-hole circuit costs 98 euros. The course includes a golf school with a driving range.

THALASSO UND THERME

What makes the *Mare Nostrum Spa (tel. 9 22 75 75 40 | www.marenostrumspa.es)* in the Mare Nostrum Resort hotel so special is its sophisticated setting and many different physiotherapy, beauty and spa treatments on 1,600 m² (17,000 sq ft).

The `INSIDER TIP` *Aqua Club Termal (daily 9am–10pm | C/ Calicia | tel. 9 22 71 65 55 | www.aquaclubtermal.com)* in Torviscas Alto has a wellness zone with hydro massages, Roman spa, seawater pool, sauna and much more. 2.5 hours cost 21 euros (cheaper rates from 8pm to 10 pm). Massages, lymph drainage and other special treatments are charged as extras.

From an atmosphere point of view, the ● *Thai Zen SPAce (daily 9am–9pm | www. elmiradorgranhotel.com)* in the Hotel El Mirador has to be the ultimate. Bathe in a minimalist-styled thalasso pool with water jets or a 25 m² (270 sq ft) jacuzzi pool. Other features include fun showers, hot-cold contrast pools and a hammam. Physiotherapists give Ayurvedic, Thai and yoga massages using only natural oils and essences from Asia.

TRAIN

A white tourist train takes sightseers on a tour of Los Cristianos and Playa de las Américas. *Daily 10am–10pm | 10 euros | departure: corner of Av. R. Puig Lluvina/Av. Santiago Puig*

ENTERTAINMENT

When the neon lights start to flicker on, treat yourself to a sundowner, stroll along the promenade or go for a bite to eat. Youngsters congregate in the *Verónica shopping centre,* the entertainment quarter along the main street near Playa de Troya, for example at the *Kaluna Beach Club.* The slightly older revellers (i.e. from age 20), on the other hand, gather in the cool music pub, the *Magic (live music daily from 10pm | Av. de las Américas | www.magicbartenerife. com).*

In the *Pirámide de Arona* (see below) there's the *Hard Rock Café (www.hardrock. com/cafes/tenerife)* with more live events. For information about the current hang-outs for gays, consult *www.gaytenerife.net.*

CASINO PLAYA DE LAS AMÉRICAS

The usual games of chance – from black-jack to roulette – are available in the basement of the Hotel Gran Tinerfe.*Mon–Thu 8pm–3am, Fri–Sun 8pm–4pm | admission free (remember to bring your passport!) | Av. del Litoral 9 | tel. 9 22 79 37 12 | www. casinostenerife.com).*

MAGMA

Pop events, classical and folk concerts are organised in this avant-garde building near the motorway. *Av. de los Pueblos | TF-1, Salida 28 | www.tenerifemagma.com*

PIRÁMIDE DE ARONA ●

Events staged in the auditorium of this imposing Las Vegas-style pyramid include `INSIDER TIP` ballet and flamenco evenings with the famous choreographer Carmen Mota, also available with dinner. *Dates in the information kiosk in Av. de las Américas | tel. 9 22 75 75 49 | www.marenostrumre-sort.com*

WHERE TO STAY

ANTHELIA

Characteristic features are a restrained elegance and first-rate fabrics in typical Mediterranean shades. Spacious garden and pool area. A very quiet hotel directly above the attractive Playa de Fañabé. *350 rooms | C/ Londres 15 | tel. 9 22 71 33 35 | www.iberostar.com | Expensive*

INSIDER TIP JARDÍN TROPICAL

Moorish architecture with little towers and minarets, two pool areas in a class of their own, beautifully planted with tall palms, plus a ⛱ viewing terrace with Bali beach chairs and a view all the way to La Gomera – you can relax in comfort. The buffets from breakfast to dinner are very good, accompanied by the background music of murmuring waterfalls. You can add a bit of variety by taking part in yoga, cooking and photography. *448 rooms and suites | C/ Gran Bretaña | San Eugenio | tel. 9 02 25 02 51 | www. jardin-tropical.com | Expensive*

EL MIRADOR ⛱

The five-star palace hotel (adults only) stands on a low cliff above the ● *Bahía del Duque,* the finest beach in the south of the island. It offers suites with a four-poster bed and a spacious natural stone bath, sea views and large flower-festooned terraces. You will be pampered from morning to night with delicious buffets; magnificent pool area descending in terraces to the beach. The orientally-themed spa is very inviting, too. Discreet, unobtrusive service and an almost intimate atmosphere. *120 rooms and suites | Av. Bruselas | tel. 9 22 71 68 68 | www.elmiradorgranhotel.com | Expensive*

PARQUE SANTIAGO III

The best in a chain of aparthotels in the south of Playa. The whitewashed residential units in Canarian style blend perfectly with the verdant gardens, pools and sunbathing lawns. Apartments and studios in different shapes and sizes. *255 apartments | Av. de las Américas | Los Morritos | tel. 9 22 74 61 03 | Budget–Moderate*

INSIDER TIP VILLA CORTÉS

Built in the style of a Mexican fort, this five-star hotel is set back from the bustling tourist resort. The Colonial design continues inside with a magnificent interior crowned with an Aztec pyramid. It also features a delightful spa and large pool garden which stretches right down to the virtually private beach. Head for the seaside beach club to watch the sunset. *151 rooms and suites | Av. Rafael Puig Lluvina 38 | tel. 9 22 75 77 00 | www.europehotels.org | Expensive*

INFORMATION

OFICINA DE TURISMO

Av. Rafael Puig Llivina 19 | Plaza de City Center | tel. 9 22 79 76 68 | www.arona. travel

OFICINA MUNICIPAL DE TURISMO

Av. Rafael Puig Lluvina 1 | next to the Artenerife shop | tel. 9 22 98 50 80 | www. costa-adeje.es

WHERE TO GO

ADEJE (144 C3) (*Ø E10*)

For most visitors, this somewhat sleepy town is just a place they travel through on the way the the "Hell's Gorge" (Barranco del Infierno). But it does have a few things of interest: At the beginning of the 16th century, the Spanish conquerors built the church of *Santa Úrsula (C/ Grande)*, with its beautifully carved coffered ceiling, here. Noble families did attend Mass, but sat in the gallery above the apse. The altarpiece for the main altar is a magnificent example of colonial Baroque. There's a tranquil ⊙ *Agromercado (Sat, Sun 8am–2pm | C/ Archajara)*, when farmers from the southern uplands come to the ● market hall to sell their produce: fruit, vegetables, goat's cheese,

Splendidly adorned carvings: the altar piece and ceiling panels of the Iglesia Santa Ursula in Adeje

aniseed bread. At the upper end of *Calle de los Molinos* the ☆ *Otelo* restaurant *(closed Tue | tel. 9 22 78 03 74 | Budget– Moderate)* boasts great views over Adeje. This is also where a beautiful hike starts: into the ☆ ★ *Barranco del Infierno (daily 8am–2:30pm (gorge open until 6pm), total hiking time approx. 3 hours | admission 8 euros, 15 euros with tour | www.barrancodelinfierno.es)*. Access only with prior reservation online or at the information stand at the entrance to the gorge | max. 300 people/day | helmets mandatory (can be hired) due to the danger of falling rocks. A narrow path, formerly used by shepherds, winds its way up into the barren mountains. There is no shade, so make sure you have some form of head protection. Later on, as you approach the narrow, shaded "Hell's Gorge" with its meandering stream, the vegetation becomes less sparse. When you reach the end of the gorge, you might be able to admire a waterfall that drops over 80 m (260 ft).

ARONA (145 D4) (*ω E–F10*)

Overshadowed by the huge Roque del Conde, it is hard to believe that this sleepy town is the administrative centre responsible for the two seemingly inexhaustible gold mines of Los Cristianos and Playa de Las Américas. Of the many billions of euros that tourism brings to the region, very little of it is spent in Arona, but it does boast an attractive town hall beside a square shaded by laurels. Beside it stands a church dating from 1627.

For tourists wishing to spend more time in the town, there are a few attractive hotels higher up, notably the ◉ *Ecohotel La Correa (6 rooms | Camino de San Antonio 58 | tel. 9 22 72 60 69 | Moderate)*, a rustic farmhouse on a green hillside run according to good environmental guidelines. The room to choose, if you get the chance, would be one of the three suites in the annexe, which overlooks almond trees and the mountains. Some 7.5 km (4.5 miles) north of Arona is the *El Nogal* hotel *(39 rooms |*

Camino Real La Escalona | tel. 9 22 72 60 50 | www.hotelnogal.com | Moderate), which occupies a country house dating from the 18th century. Since that time, it has been in the Linares family, who also run a good restaurant here. Old floorboards and beamed ceilings help to create an intimate atmosphere; there's an indoor pool and a sauna.

LA CALETA (144 C4) (*m D10*)

Once a quiet fishing village overlooking the new resorts in the distance, La Caleta has long since been swallowed up itself by tourism: its luxury hotels and golf course provide the evidence as does the pedestrian-only promenade which you can use to walk to Los Cristianos.

The most charming accommodation is located 2 km inland next to the resort's golf course built in the style of a typical Canarian village. The **INSIDER TIP** *Royal Garden Villas (C/ Alcojora | tel. 9 22 71 12 94 | www.royalgardenvillas.com | Expensive)* offer luxurious and intimate surroundings – each of the 28 spacious villas has its own pool and large terrace. Breakfast in this lush five-star residence is served in the *Restaurant Jardín (Moderate–Expensive)* eingenommen. And if it should rain, try the spa instead of the sea. La Caleta's fish restaurants have survived, yet these former rustic eateries have been transformed into large, comfortable restaurants. Right by the water's edge is the *La Caleta* restaurant *(daily | tel. 9 22 78 06 75 | Moderate)*. The open balcony above the rocks is a great place to dine. A wide selection of tapas, meat and fish included on a long menu. Unfortunately, the quality of the meat dishes varies. The terrace restaurant *La Masía del Mar & Piscis (daily | C/ del Muelle 3 | tel. 9 22 71 08 95 | www.masiadelmar. com | Moderate)* next door has a better reputation: the sumptuous fish soup is served in small copper pots, and you can have your seafood freshly caught in the restaurant's aquarium.

PLAYA PARAÍSO (144 B3) (*m D10*)

The name "paradise beach" is an awful exaggeration. But it still has a small bay for swimming with golden sand and another with dark sand. The resort's eye-catcher is a twin tower: *the Hard Rock Hotel (624 rooms | Av. de Adeje | tel. 9 71 92 76 91 | www.hardrockhotels.com/ tenerife | Expensive)*. stylish, without flogging the musical theme too much to death. There you'll find a Rock Spa, a gym called Body Rock, three large pools and a wide range of sporting activities. **INSIDER TIP** The Sky Lounge Bar on the 16th floor offers a great view.

SAN JUAN/PLAYA DE ALCALÁ (144 A–B2) (*m C9*)

Emerging like a rusty mirage outside the resort of San Juan, the ⭐ *Abama (450 rooms and garden suites | location: TF-47, 9 km/5 miles | tel. 9 22 12 60 00 | www. abamahotelresort.com | Expensive)*, a

San Juan and Alcalá seem so out-of-the-way – and yet there are two five-star hotels here

huge luxury resort in Moroccan kasbah style. It even has its own golf course. There are villa complexes at several levels running right down to the sea. A park, seven pools, a spa, nine restaurants, a funicular down to the bright bathing cove – everything here is simply the best.

From the thoroughfare San Juan appears somewhat dull yet head to the harbour which has retained some of the town's flair with an attractive artificial sandy beach, promenade and restaurant pavilions. Appetizing tapas with daily specials are served on the village square at *San Juan Creativo (Plaza de la Iglesia | mobile tel. 6 50 60 97 91 | Budget)*. The goat's cheese with local honey is delicious.

The Palacio de Isora resort hotel *(609 rooms and suites | tel. 9 22 86 90 00 | www.melia.com | Expensive)* in Alcalá is the sort of place that sets benchmarks. This vast complex in southern Spanish style is situated by a rocky beach with views of La Gomera. Great seawater pool with jacuzzis, gardens, five restaurants and bistros, various bars, discos

and luxurious designer rooms, plus a first-class spa.

Its counterpart is the small, family-run *Hotel Rural El Navio (Prolongación Av. Los Pescadores | tel. 9 22 86 56 80 | www. elnavio.es | Moderate)*, situated 2 km (1.2 miles) away from the resort in the middle of a banana plantation. Pomp is replaced with rustic charm, rural surroundings, peace and tranquillity. With only 14 rooms, you quickly get to know the other guests over breakfast or at the small pool.

PUERTO DE SANTIAGO

(140 B–C5) *(ﾉﾉ C8)* **This was once just the small fishing village of Puerto de Santiago. But the tourism boom added two new developments to it: Playa de las Arenas is named after the eponymous lava beach and Los Gigantes after the "gigantic" cliffs that shoot up 450 m (1,500 ft) from the water in**

the north. The marvellous landscape stands in contrast with row upon row of identical often joyless giant hotels.

But ⭐ *Playa de la Arena*, a 300 m (1,000 ft) long beach with fine, jet-black volcanic sand contrasting bright green palm trees, is lovely. The beach is the island's sunniest spot and has regularly been awarded with the European Blue Flag for the cleanliness of its water and sand. It also has excellent facilities with sun loungers (to hire), toilets and lifeguards.

FOOD & DRINK

CASA PANCHO

This beach restaurant at Playa de las Arenas offers fine cuisine and has won several awards. The grilled fish is tasty, as is the duck breast in honey sauce. And if you want to treat yourself, order the `INSIDER TIP` excellent six-course menu of the season for 40 euros. *Closed Mon | Av. Marítima 26 | tel. 9 22 86 13 23 | casapancho.info | Moderate*

DELI ON THE HILL

Fresh salads, snacks, sandwiches and homemade cake served in a pleasant atmosphere: a good spot to take a break. *Closed Sun | Ctra. General Puerto Santiago 32 | mobile tel. 6 28 50 01 63 | www.delionthehill.eu | Budget*

EL RINCÓN DE JUAN CARLOS

A gem in this place? Hidden in a courtyard behind the Los Gigantes church? Yes! Here, the gastronomy professionals of the Padrón family make creative Canarian dishes that are both delicious and visually stunning. They do this without a trace a trace of stress. As a customer, you'll be infected with the relaxed mood right away. *Only evenings, closed Sun | Pasaje Jacaranda 2 | tel. 9 22 86 80 40 | www. elrincondejuancarlos.com | Expensive (menus starting from 55 euros)*

In luck – a pilot whale has come up for air: whale watching off the coast of Los Gigantes

WHERE TO STAY

LUABAY COSTA LOS GIGANTES ☆

An all-inclusive resort on a cliff-top. 518 family-friendly, sea view suites with living room and bedroom, so ideal for two adults with children. For the children there's a games room, cinema, pool with water slide, mini-disco and a special buffet. *C/ Juan Manuel Capdevielle 8 | tel. 9 22 86 72 72 | www.belivehotels.com | Moderate*

INFORMATION

OFICINA DE TURISMO

Centro Comercial Seguro el Sol | C/ Manuel Ravelo 20 | tel. 9 22 86 03 48 | www.santiagodelteide.org | www.losgigantes.com

WHERE TO GO

LOS GIGANTES ★ (140 B5) (*ω C8*)

"The Giants" is the name of the spectacular steep cliffs at the end of the coastal road, 1 km (0.6 miles) to the north. The cliff face drops 450 m (1,500 ft) vertically into the sea. Los Gigantes is also the name of the seaside resort with narrow streets nestled alongside the rocks. On the water you'll find the calm *Poblado Marinero (93 apartments | C/ Los Guíos | tel. 9 22 86 09 66 | www.pobladomarinero.com | Budget)*, a quarter inspired by a fishing village. The black-sand beach, 200 m (660 ft) long *Playa de los Guíos* begins here. It's wonderfully situated at the foot of the cliffs, but there is a danger of falling rocks – so it might be a good idea to put your towel down closer to the water. The most beautiful view of the cliffs can be enjoyed from the ☆ marina with its rows of swinging yachts. Los Gigantes are even more impressive, when viewed from a boat which takes you right up to the cliffs. The former shrimper "Katrin" is just one of a number of boats that take sightseers out for INSIDER TIP *dolphin watching (daily from 11:30am | 2-hour trip 25 euros | 100 m (330 ft)* before the harbour entrance on the right | tel. 9 22 86 03 32). The catamaran "Nashiro Uno" organises one- to three-hour whale and dolphin watching tours from the harbour *(daily from 10:45am, 1:45pm and 4pm | 20–40 euros, depending on the duration | www.maritimaacantilados.com)*. More than 25 species of marine mammals can be spotted off the coast of Tenerife. The ones most commonly seen on the trips are long-finned pilot whales and bottle-nose dolphins.

GUÍA DE ISORA (141 D6) (*ω D8*)

In this town, 10 km (6 miles) southeast of Puerto de Santiago, many employees that work in the resorts live in cheap, purpose-built buildings. If you want to see the nicer side of Guía de Isora (pop. 5,200), head for the historical centre above the thoroughfare. The handsome *Iglesia Nuestra Señora de la Luz* at the church square is a reminder that a lot of wealth was created here in the 16th century. If you have a penchant for unusual delicacies then make a short detour to Chío. In the wonderful INSIDER TIP ◎ *Delicias del Sol* shop *(Mon–Fri 10am–3pm, Sat 10am–2pm | on the main street in Chío, TF-82 32.5 km/20 miles | www.deliciasdelsol.eu)* you can buy jams and chutneys made from ● exotic fruits, mojo sauces in every flavour, fig and walnut cakes, organic wines and liqueurs, as well as wholegrain breads and pastries. Starting above Guías is one of three access roads to Teide National Park, ☆ a magnificent car journey, first through farmland and then across a barren volcanic region at an altitude of 2,000m (6,500ft).

DISCOVERY TOURS

① TENERIFE AT A GLANCE

START: ① Puerto de la Cruz
END: ① Puerto de la Cruz

Distance:
🚗 260 km/161 miles

2 days
Driving time
(without stops)
7 hours

COSTS: For 2 people: 260 euros for hire car, petrol, food, accommodation and cable car

WHAT TO PACK: Sun cream, headwear, warm jacket, swimwear

IMPORTANT TIPS: Progress is slow on mountain roads.
As most visitors arrive at the national park and the Mount Teide cable car around noon, it is recommended to set off early.

This tour takes you through all the island's climatic zones on the way up to Spain's highest mountain, Mount Teide. First through a lush green landscape, you then

Would you like to explore the places that are unique to this island? Then the Discovery Tours are just the thing for you – they include terrific tips for stops worth making, breathtaking places to visit, selected restaurants and fun activities. It's even easier with the Touring App: download the tour with map and route to your smartphone using the QR Code on pages 2/3 or from the website address in the footer below – and you'll never get lost again even when you're offline.

→ p. 2/3

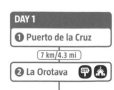

ascend to windy heights where there are no trees in sight. Las Cañadas' gigantic crater with its rock formations rises up dramatically – and remnants of old and new volcanic eruptions are evident everywhere. In contrast are the lively towns of La Orotava and La Laguna as well as the sun-bathed beaches along the southern coast.

Start in ❶ **Puerto de la Cruz** → p. 44 **and head south** through the densely populated **Valle de la Orotava** → p. 41 first to the picturesque village of ❷ **La Orotava** → p. 41. Romantic plazas, churches and monasteries serve as reminders of the island's colonial past.

DAY 1

❶ Puerto de la Cruz

7 km/4.3 mi

❷ La Orotava

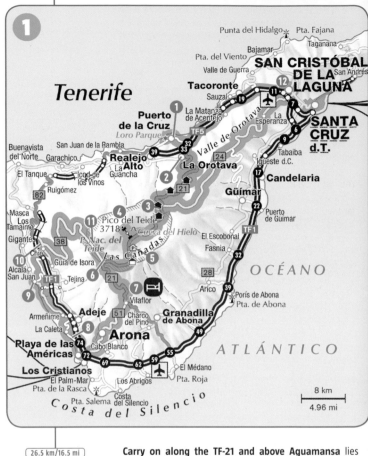

Tenerife

Punta del Hidalgo · Pta. Fajana
Bajamar · Taganana
Pta. del Viento
Valle de Guerra
SAN CRISTÓBAL DE LA LAGUNA · San Andrés
Tacoronte
Sauzal
La Matanza de Acentejo
1 **Puerto de la Cruz**
Loro Parque
TF5
Realejo Alto
La Guancha
San Juan de la Rambla
Buenavista del Norte
Garachico
El Tanque
Icod de los Vinos
Ruigómez
82
La Orotava
21
La Esperanza
SANTA CRUZ d.T.
Tabaiba
Igueste d.C.
17
Candelaria
Güímar
Puerto de Güímar
22
TF1
El Escobonal
Fasnia
32
28
Arico
39
Porís de Abona
Pta. de Abona
Masca
Los Tamaimos
Gigantes
38
Chio
Guía de Isora
21
Pico del Teide
3718
P. Nac. del Teide
Cueva del Hielo
Las Cañadas
5
11
6
Tejina
OCÉANO
10
Alcalá
San Juan
TF1
9
Armeñime
La Caleta
Adeje
8
Playa de las Américas
74
72
Los Cristianos
El Palm-Mar
Pta. de la Rasca
69
7
51
Charco del Pino
Cabo Blanco
Arona
62
Los Abrigos
Costa del Silencio
Pta. Salema
Costa del Silencio
Granadilla de Abona
49
59
55
El Médano
Pta. Roja
ATLÁNTICO
Vilaflor
Valle de Orotava
24
2
3
32
33
39

8 km
4.96 mi

(26.5 km/16.5 mi)

Carry on along the TF-21 and above Aguamansa lies the green crater **La Caldera → p. 44**, now a picnic area and starting point for hiking tours into the pine forest. Between the 22 and 23 km markers, stop to take a look at the natural phenomenon **La Margarita de Piedra** (Stone Rose), a large basalt rosette, the remains of volcanic eruptions.

At an altitude of 2,000m (6,562 ft) the forest thins and volcanic rock dominates the landscape. The gateway to the Las Cañadas crater and the **National Park → p. 68**, **3 El Portillo → p. 71**, an attractive visitor centre, presents itself. A rock garden contains all the plants that have adapted to

3 El Portillo

the extreme alpine climate; the finest is the Mount Teide bugloss, a perennial that grows to a height of about 2m (6.5 ft) and sports a mass of reddish flowers. As the road continues, the landscape varies between lava and ash fields in white, green, red, grey and pitch black. They bear witness to the volcanic activity, which shaped the island millions of years ago. **At the 43 km marker, you'll reach the turn-off to the cable car station** to take the cable car which goes from 2,300 m (7,546 ft) up to 3,555 m (11,663 ft) in a few minutes to the **④ mountain station** of **Mount Teide → p. 70**, the 3,718m (12,198 ft.) high mountain. The panoramic view from the top is amazing!

The next break is at the **Roques de García → p. 70**, giant weathered rock formations that tower above a crater framed by jagged rock walls. The nearby **⑤ Parador Nacional → p. 70**, is the perfect place to take a break with either its cafeteria or rustic restaurant *(Budget–Moderate)* – both offering impressive views of the Teide. The following make spectacular vantage points: the 5 m (16 ft) high **Zapato de la Reina**, or "Queen's Shoe", then the **⑥ Boca de Tauce**, a breach in the caldera rim. **You now leave Las Cañadas crater and follow the TF-21** down through the sparse pine forest to **⑦ Vilaflor → p. 76**, a mountain village at a height of almost 1,500 m (4,921 ft). Enjoy a hearty meal at **Rincón del Roberto, → p. 77** before spending the night in the alpine hotel **Spa Villalba → p. 77**.

While Vilaflor is often hidden in the clouds, the village of **Arona → p. 91** just **12 km (7.5 miles) away i**s often bathed in light from the south. Now leave the mountain landscape behind and head for Tenerife's tourist centre. Make your way to the coast where a 16 km (9.9 mile) promenade links the coastal resorts together, from Los Cristianos to La Caleta. There are beaches every few hundred metres along the promenade – the finest being the **⑧ Bahía del Duque** overlooked by some spectacular hotels. There are some excellent fish restaurants in La Caleta → p. 92, but try and wait to eat until you reach **⑨ San Juan → p. 92,** a quiet fishing and coastal village with its row of harbour restaurants.

After your meal, **take the TF-463 up to Chío** where you can purchase some of the island's delicacies at **⑩ Delicias del Sol → p. 95 (TF-82 at 32.5 km marker)**. You'll then encounter some splendid natural beauty: The TF-38 takes you through volcanic landscape with pine trees. From the

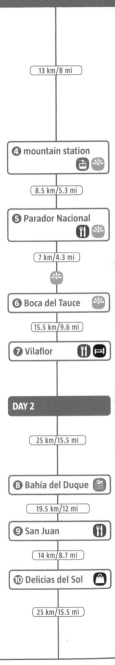

13 km/8 mi

④ mountain station

8.5 km/5.3 mi

⑤ Parador Nacional

7 km/4.3 mi

⑥ Boca del Tauce

15.5 km/9.6 mi

⑦ Vilaflor

DAY 2

25 km/15.5 mi

⑧ Bahía del Duque

19.5 km/12 mi

⑨ San Juan

14 km/8.7 mi

⑩ Delicias del Sol

25 km/15.5 mi

⑪ Mirador Chío ☀

⑪ Mirador Chío you can look out across fields of black clinker to the **Pico Viejo → p. 68**, Mount Teide's younger brother. At the Boca de Tauce **you'll meet again the TF-21 high mountain road** which is so spectacular that you won't mind returning along it in the opposite direction.

On the return journey from El Portillo take the TF-24 across the island's backbone. After a few kilometres, you'll pass by the entrance to the domes of the **Observatorio del Teide → p. 71, and at the 32 km marker you will pass** several black-white-yellow rock formations known as **La Tarta**, "the cake". After that you are back in the pine forest. Where the woodland thins out, you will find a series of viewpoints. Sometimes you look east, sometimes northwest, sometimes you see the neighbouring island of La Palma, sometimes Gran Canaria.

After so much natural beauty, it's now time for a spot of culture: **⑫ La Laguna → p. 55**, a Unesco World Heritage site, is a picture-book town with cobbled, pedestrianised streets lined by churches, monasteries and palaces. A hearty meal can be enjoyed at **La Maquila → p. 56**. From La Laguna, **take the TF-5 motorway** back to **❶ Puerto de la Cruz** to take an early evening swim. The pitch black "garden beach" **Playa Jardín → p. 49** is the perfect place for a dip while enjoying the sunset view. Then relax over a cocktail in one of the palmshaded beach bars

`71.5 km/44 mi`

🏢

☀

⑫ La Laguna 🏙 🍴

`29.5 km/18 mi`

❶ Puerto de la Cruz 🏖 🍹

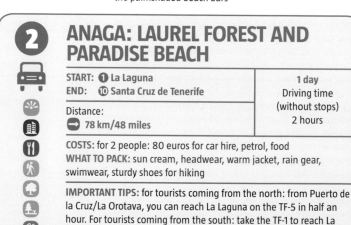

2 ANAGA: LAUREL FOREST AND PARADISE BEACH

🚗
☀
🏢
🍴
🚶
🌳
🏛
🌊

START: ❶ La Laguna	1 day
END: ⑩ Santa Cruz de Tenerife	Driving time (without stops)
Distance: ➡ 78 km/48 miles	2 hours

COSTS: for 2 people: 80 euros for car hire, petrol, food
WHAT TO PACK: sun cream, headwear, warm jacket, rain gear, swimwear, sturdy shoes for hiking

IMPORTANT TIPS: for tourists coming from the north: from Puerto de la Cruz/La Orotava, you can reach La Laguna on the TF-5 in half an hour. For tourists coming from the south: take the TF-1 to reach La Laguna in 1.5 hours.

Alongside the national park and the Teno mountains, the Anaga mountain range is almost virgin territory in Tenerife. Many of the steep wooded slopes are totally inaccessible. That's a good thing for the laurel forest. It has survived here; elsewhere it would have been wiped out. A few secluded hamlets have survived on various rocky outcrops, plus one or two fishing villages down at the coast which can only be reached along long serpentine roads.

09:30am The tour starts in **❶ La Laguna** → p. 55 **where you take the TF-12 INSIDERTIP panoramic road** to Las Mercedes where the laurel forest begins. **At the 25.1 km marker,** it's worth making a stop at the **❷ Mirador de Jardina**, from where you can survey over half the island as far as Mount Teide. Soon after **at the 22.7 km marker,** you will reach the **❸ Mirador Cruz del Carmen** where a well-camouflaged **visitor centre** → p. 59, will supply you with information about all the walking trails in the region. Even a one-hour easy walking tour provides you with a good insight into the laurel forest. Cruz del Carmen also has a tiny chapel and the rustic bistro **La Gangochera** → p. 59 Continue along the road and the next viewpoint **at the 21.8 km marker,** the **❹ Mirador Pico del Inglés** provides a different vista down over the northwest and northeast coasts.

You can leave the TF-12 at various points to explore lonely hamlets, such as Las Carboneras, Chinamada or Taborno.

At the natural beach at Benijo in the northeast of Tenerife, you can only swim at low tide

⑤ Casas de Afur

14 km / 8.7 mi

⑥ Bailadero

9.5 km / 5.9 mi

⑦ Casa África

2 km / 1.25 mi

⑧ Benijo

⑤ Casas de Afur is especially quaint **(fork at the 18.4 km marker)**. Continue along the high mountain road and at km 11.4 you'll reach a chaotic junction. **Head in the direction of ⑥ Bailadero**, where sheep and goats were once rounded up. **2.4 km (1.5 miles) further – on the TF-123 – exit the high mountain road and continue along the TF-134 towards "Taganana/Benijo".** The road now drops down in sweeping bends past sharply-defined ridges to enjoy magnificent views of the cliffs below and the landscape around. You'll be tempted to park up along the way to enjoy these views yet there are very few parking opportunities along this narrow ridge...

01:00pm After this spectacular route at dizzying heights, you've earned your fish lunch on this rocky coastline; restaurants offering great views of the wild surf can be found in **Roque de las Bodegas**, for example the authentic Canarian **⑦ Casa África** *(daily | Roque de las Bodegas 3 | tel. 9 22 59 01 00 | Budget–Moderate)* where the friendly Señora África cooks up traditional specialities and in **⑧ Benijo** with its pretty beach.

`03:30pm` After visiting Benijo turn round and **head back up to the mountains**, and from the spine of the Anaga Mountains it is now downhill once more **along the serpentine road to the east side of the island** and the fishing and seaside resort of **⑨ San Andrés** → p. 65. You can have a `INSIDER TIP` bite to eat here and enjoy a long swim at Tenerife's finest beach. Now head along the coast to the capital **⑩ Santa Cruz de Tenerife** → p. 60 Follow signs to La Laguna for the north coast or take the TF-1 motorway to the resorts in the south.

| 18 km/11 mi |

⑨ San Andrés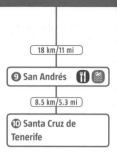

| 8.5 km/5.3 mi |

⑩ Santa Cruz de Tenerife

③ TENO: STEEP GORGES AND PICTURESQUE RESORTS

START: ① Los Gigantes	1 day
END: ① Los Gigantes	Driving time
	(without stops)
Distance:	2 hours
🚗 120 km/74.5 miles	

COSTS: for 2 people: 90 euros for hire car, petrol, food
WHAT TO PACK: sun cream, headwear, warm jacket, swimwear, sturdy shoes for the walk around Masca

IMPORTANT TIPS: The TF-445 to ⑤ **Punta de Teno** is officially closed in strong winds and rain due to the danger of falling rocks. A bus shuttle is provided on weekends.

Rising up in the far northwest is the Teno Massif, a mountain range with adventurous ridges and jagged peaks. The few inhabitants of this rugged region live in tiny villages carved into the rock. Head to the coast to discover another side of this region: you can expect to see the splendid Garachico, a "thousand-year old" dragon tree and one of the world's longest volcanic tunnels.

`09:00am` **① Los Gigantes** → p. 95, known as the "Giants", are striking rocky cliffs which rise to 450 m (1,500 ft) above the village of the same name. They dwarf the houses, boats and people around. Los Gigantes are located at the southern end of the Teno Massif and foreshadow the inaccessible mountains which you are now driving towards. **The TF-454 first climbs through hairpin bends on its way up to Santiago del Teide,** passing banana and tomato plantations. **At km 11, make a detour to**

① Los Gigantes

| 14.5 km/9 mi |

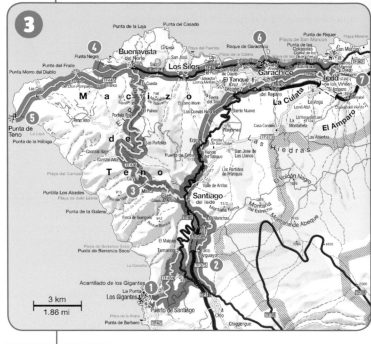

3

Punta de la Laja · Punta del Casado
Punta del Riquel
Playa de San Marcos · Playa Moreno
Punta de la Costa · Playa del Puertito · Roque de Garachico · **6** · Punta de las Cotorrillas · San Marcos
Punta Negra · **4** · Buenavista del Norte · San José · Los Silos · Garachico · Icod · **7**
Punta del Fraile · La Cuesta · TF-445 · Mirador Lomo Molino · El Tanque · Cruz del Reparo · Cuevas del Viento
Punta Morro del Diablo · La Caleta · Las Cuevas Negras · La Culata · La Vega · El Amparo
M a c i z o · Teno Alto · Portela Baja · Tierra del Trigo · Barrio Nuevo · Casa Canales · La Montañeta · Las Abiertas
5 · Punta de Teno · La Laya · Las Portelas · Puerto de Erjos · Erjos · San José de Los Llanos · El Volcán Negro · **L a s   H i e d r a s**
Punta de la Hábiga · Carrizal Bajo · Ermita de San Isidro · Los Partidos de Franquis
Playa del Carrizal · Carrizal Alto · **T e n o** · Valle de Arriba · Santiago del Teide · Montaña del Estrecho · Montaña de Abeque
Puntilla Los Abades · Playa de Juan López · **3** · Masca · Montaña Bilma · Las Manchas
Punta de la Galera · Finca de Guergues · Roque Blanco · El Malpaís
Playa de Berrugo Seco · Tamaimo · **2** · Arguayo
Punta de Berrugo Seco · La Canaria
Acantilado de los Gigantes · **1** · Los Gigantes · La Punta · Puerto de Santiago · Chío · Chiguergue
Playa de la Arena · Punta de Barbero

3 km
1.86 mi

2 Arguayo 🏛 🛍

11 km/6.8 mi

3 Masca 🚶 🍴

2 Arguayo → p. 37. In this village with its long pottery tradition, an old **ceramic workshop** has been restored and visitors are welcome to watch the skilled potters at work and purchase their products.

After passing Santiago del Teide → p. 37, the landscape becomes more dramatic: steep cliffs everywhere you look, rugged rocks and occasional plants. The **Teno Mountains → p. 36** is geologically a very old formation where erosion has gnawed away at the volcanic rock. From the **Mirador de Cherfe** you get your first glimpse of **3 Masca → p. 36**, below, a hamlet set between sheer rock walls which until the 1980s managed without any road connection to the outside world. It is divided between several rocky outcrops and a tour through this dispersed village will involve treading carefully on crooked cobblestones; small bars and cafés are available offering drinks and snacks. **For a few kilometres, the narrow ribbon of asphalt winds its way through the mountain range.** At the **Mirador de Hilda** with its panorama terrace and café, you have a splendid view of the Masca valley behind you before the next pass where the **Mirador**

de Baracán, offers a view of the gentler hills in the north. **Then drive through the village Las Portelas heading down to Buenavista del Norte → p. 36** where you can enjoy excellent fish cuisine at the coastal restaurant **④ El Burgado** *(daily | Playa de las Arenas | tel. 9 02 09 17 55 | Moderate)*.

01:30pm **From Buenavista the secluded TF-445 now runs along the rocky coastline in the far northwest corner of Tenerife.** Take care when the weather is bad! Rockfalls are not uncommon after heavy rain. **The journey comes to an end at the cape ⑤ Punta de Teno → p. 36,** where you can jump into the waves in a protected bay at the foot of the high cliffs around. After so much untrammelled nature, you will soon find yourself in a friendly place. **Back in Buenavista, continue driving for five minutes until you reach ⑥ Garachico → p. 33.** A fort, monastery and colonial houses form the Old Town, a splendid example of Tenerife's traditional architecture. The lava rock coast is also worth a look – you can enjoy the view over a meal on the terrace of **El Caletón** *(daily | Av. Tome Cano | tel. 9 22 13 33 01 | Moderate)*.

19 km/11.8 mi

④ El Burgado

10 km/6.2 mi

⑤ Punta de Teno

18.5 km/11.5 mi

⑥ Garachico

5.5 km/3.4 mi

Beautiful hamlet in an impressive mountain landscape: Masca

⑦ Icod de los Vinos

(15.5 km / 9.6 mi)

① Los Gigantes

04:00pm After your well-earned break, **continue on the TF-42 to ⑦ Icod de los Vinos → p. 38,** where you will find the Drago Milenario, a dragon tree believed to be 1000 years old and one of Tenerife's most recognised landmarks. It is fun to stroll down the nearby historic streets lined with stately homes. Have a free glass of wine in one of the **culinary shops. Now head back in the direction of Puerto de Santiago** along a less dramatic but just as beautiful mountain road through El Tanque, Erjos and Santiago del Teide to your starting point at **① Los Gigantes.**

4

HIKE TO THE ROQUES DE GARCÍA

START: ① Mirador de la Ruleta **END:** ① Mirador de la Ruleta	**4 hours** Hiking time (without stops) 1 ¾ hours
Distance: medium	
🚶 4.5 km/ 2.8 miles .ıl **difference in altitude:** 110 m/361 ft	

COSTS: 20 euros per person for food
WHAT TO PACK: sturdy shoes, sun protection, drinking water

IMPORTANT: From Puerto de la Cruz, take bus 348 leaving at 9:15am. From Las Américas, take bus 342 to the end stop at Parador. Return journey around 4pm.
By car, take the TF-21 and at the 46.4 km marker park up at the Mirador de la Ruleta or alternatively at the car park at Parador.
Do not leave anything in your car!
Take sufficient amount of drinking water with you!
Hike in the mornings or afternoons when the sun is lower.

This tour is relatively easy and still spectacular: past the rugged gigantic rocks, also called "God's Finger", "Hercules' Rocks" or the "White Tower", you then descend to the Ucanca plateau. Mount Teide always appears in close reach with rugged rocks glistening in the background and a bright azure blue sky above.

---

① Mirador de la Ruleta

(300 m / 328 yd)

② Roques de García

From your starting point at the viewpoint **① Mirador de la Ruleta,** take a few steps back **in the direction of the TF-21 and turn left immediately behind the set of rocks along a wide path signposted "Sendero 3".** The path ascends gradually past the foot of the **② Roques de García → p. 70** which have been carved out by wind and rain over the course of millions of years. The path soon narrows and

---

follows along the edge of a lava field. 30 minutes after setting off, you'll pass the **❸ Torre Blanca**, a "white tower", the last rock in the series of gigantic rock formations. A natural panorama plateau has been carved out here offering a vast view over the Ucanca plain.

Shortly after the plateau, the path takes a left and gently descends to the plain below – with the craggy foot of the Roques de García rising up in front of you. When the path becomes unclear, cairns have been used to mark out the route ahead. You'll quickly spot your next destination, the **❹ "Cathedral"**, a 100 m/ 328ft high solitary rock rising up from the plateau. This formation's vertical faces are popular with rock climbers. **Before reaching the cathedral rock, the route bends left and climbs steeply up a serpentine path** – this is the most strenuous section of the hike: the ascent over the rock back to the viewpoint **❺ Mirador de la Ruleta**. Enjoy the view here over the vast, desolate Ucanca plateau from which the giant rocks rise like prehistoric stones with the rugged walls of Las Cañadas on the horizon in the background.

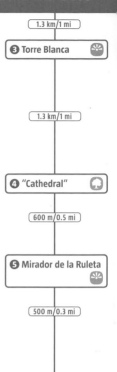

1.3 km/1 mi

❸ Torre Blanca

1.3 km/1 mi

❹ "Cathedral"

600 m/0.5 mi

❺ Mirador de la Ruleta

500 m/0.3 mi

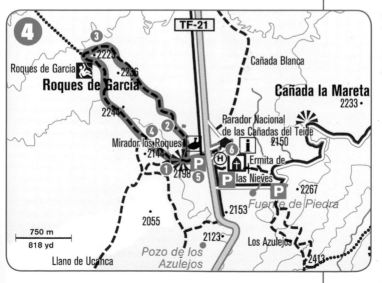

6 Parador Nacional 🍴 ☀

500 m/0.3 mi

1 Mirador de la Ruleta

Now it's time for food and refreshment! **Head on the access road to the Mirador until you reach the TF-21, cross the road and go directly** to the pale violet building of the **6** **Parador Nacional** → p. 70 After a further 450 m (164 ft) on foot, you'll reach the cafeteria for a snack or the rustic restaurant for Canarian specialities while taking one long last look at Mount Teide before heading back to your starting point at the **1** **Mirador de la Ruleta**.

Resting spot in front of splendid scenery: Parador Nacional centre beneath the Teide

5 CYCLING TOUR IN THE SOUTHERN MOUNTAIN LANDSCAPE

START: ❶ Los Cristianos END: ❶ Los Cristianos	1 day Cycling time (without stops) 6 hours
Distance: 🚴 65 km/40 miles	Difficulty: 📶 medium	

COSTS: Per person: mountain bikes from 16 euros, admission to **Jungle Park** and **Mariposa sculpture park** 25 euros per person, admission incl. guided tour ❿ **Reserva Ambiental** 15 euros; coffee, drinks and food 35 euros

WHAT TO PACK: drinking water for the first strenuous stage, swimwear

IMPORTANT TIPS: road/mountain bike hire (including helmets) in Las Américas at Diga Sports → p. 112. It's the law in Spain to wear bike helmets! Reserve in advance to visit the **Mariposa sculpture park** *(only Tue and Thu | tel. 922 726 232)* and a 2-hour guided tour at the **Reserva Ambiental San Blas** *(tel. 922 749 010 | www.sandos.com)*. If you want to skip the first strenuous section of this tour, take bus 480 in Los Cristianos to Arona (no extra charge for transporting bikes in buses).

An imposing mountainside extending from the southern coast towards Mount Teide across a barren volcanic region. You'll encounter on your route historical villages where inhabitants have lived off the land for centuries – get ready to experience the traditional, rural face of Tenerife! The tour is only strenuous at the start: after a gradual ascent of 600 metres (1,968 feet), the route levels out and after a dramatic downhill stretch from Granadilla to the coast, you return to your starting point along a relatively even section.

Leave ❶ **Los Cristianos** → p. 79 **on the TF-665 (signposted Chayofa/ Arona). After the motorway roundabout, take the TF-28** finally leaving the town behind you. Traffic becomes less and the scenery more rural. Although you'll have to start pedalling harder uphill, you'll be leaving the sprawl of the coastal tourist resorts safely behind you. Take a first coffee break in ❷ **Chayofa** where foreign residents live in their flowery bungalows. **Mesón Chayofa** *(daily | C/ El Taroso 43 | tel. 922 72 91 89 | Moderate)* offers food and refreshment in quiet surroundings in what used to be a tomato plantation; another attraction is the **Jungle Park** *(daily 10am–5:30pm | www.aguilasjunglepark.com)* with tigers, sea lions, monkeys

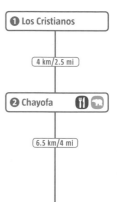

❶ Los Cristianos

4 km/2.5 mi

❷ Chayofa

6.5 km/4 mi

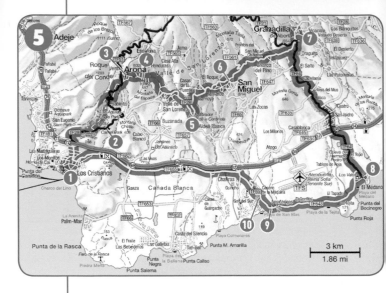

❸ Arona 🛁

1 km/0.6 mi

❹ Túnez ⓘ

5.5 km/3.5 mi

❺ Mirador de la Centinela 🍽️🍴

4.5 km/2.8 mi

❻ San Miguel 🏛️🏠

5.5 km/3.4 mi

❼ Granadilla de Abona 🏛️🏠☕

and a birds of prey show. **From here, continue along a road which runs parallel to the TF-51 where you'll reach** the 630 m (2,067 ft) high municipality of **❸ Arona → p. 91** surmounted by a pyramid mountain. It boasts an attractive plaza with town hall, church and dense laurel trees where you can take a well-earned break beneath the trees' shade. You then head towards **❹ Túnez along a side road** where two gallery owners have created a 2 ha (5 acre) art and sculpture park **INSIDERTIP Mariposa** *(C/ Túnez 63-A)*.

In Valle de San Lorenzo, you return to the TF-28 and, after a few kilometres, you reach the **❺ Mirador de la Centinela**, the finest panoramic view in the island's south: you can enjoy the fantastic view in the panoramic restaurant **Centinela** *(Closed Mon | Budget–Moderate)*. Without any steep ascents and over gentle rolling hills, the route continues to **❻ San Miguel**, with its pretty church, cobbled streets and the ethnic museum **Casa del Capitán** *(Closed Sat/Sun | C/ Calvario 1)* 4 km (2.5 miles) away lies **❼ Granadilla de Abona**, a community which witnessed heavy expansion in the boom years. Head to its historic core to experience its nostalgic charm. Alongside the parish church, the former post office is also worth visiting which has been transformed today into the rustic **Hotel Rural Senderos de Abona** *(C/ Peatonal de la Iglesia 5 | www.senderosdeabona.es | Budget)*. Besides the restaurant's café terrace, the hotel also features a **curiosity cabinet** with many useful objects collected over the ages.

Past Granadilla, follow the well-earned stretch downhill: **On the TF-64 you'll gain speed and continue 7.5 km (5 miles) to the coast, over the TF-1 motorway until you reach ❽ El Médano →** p. 84 **5 km (3 miles) away.** This is Tenerife's surfer paradise with the longest natural sandy beach on the island: it stretches 3 km (1.9 miles) in the shadow of the Red Mountain (Montaña Roja). Take a dip in the waves! You can enjoy a relaxing swim at the **Playa de la Tejita →** p. 85, situated to the west of the Red Mountain.

After a refreshing swim, **continue on the TF-643** along the coast to the next attraction: there are rows of restaurants and bars offering fresh sea food around the harbour of **Los Abrigos →** p. 83 for example at the ❾ **Perlas del Mar →** p. 83. After your meal, it's now time to soak in some culture: Visit the ❿ **Reserva Ambiental**. **In the canyon behind the five-star resort San Blas (Av. Greñamora 1) to** the west of Los Abrigos, you can immerse yourself in the magical tuff landscape – including a trip on a mini boat. An interactive **Museum** also offers an insight into Tenerife's nature and history. **On the TF-655 head back to ❶ Los Cristianos** – it's easy driving along the flat coastal terrain!

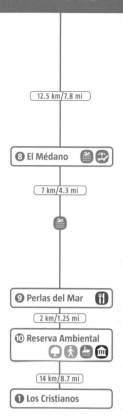

| 12.5 km / 7.8 mi |

❽ El Médano

| 7 km / 4.3 mi |

❾ Perlas del Mar

| 2 km / 1.25 mi |

❿ Reserva Ambiental

| 14 km / 8.7 mi |

❶ Los Cristianos

Rustic and pleasant: the Granadilla Hotel Rural Senderos de Abona

SPORTS & ACTIVITIES

As the northeast trade winds sweep reliably along Tenerife's coasts, windsurfing is the most popular of the many different water sports. Bodysurfing off Playa de las Américas has become very popular too.

But there are plenty of outdoor activities to do on land too – trail running, hiking and biking, climbing, paragliding, golf... Agencies in the resort towns hire out equipment and offer courses for all levels of experience. And the biggest sporting event? That would be the *Vuelta Ciclista* – the round-the-island cycle race in September.

CYCLING

Among elite professional road racers, Tenerife has become very popular because of the steep hill climbs and the mild winter climate. Leisure cyclists will find flat roads by the coast, but they will have to share the highways with a lot of traffic. Please note: a helmet is compulsory for cyclists in Spain. Mountain-bikers are allowed to go off-road.

If you are in one of the holiday resorts, to hire a cycle for a day will cost from 13 euros, for a week from 95 euros, e.g. from *Diga Sports (Av. Rafael Puig 23 | Playa de las Américas | tel. 9 22 79 30 09 | www.digasports.co.uk.)* Guided tours start at 40 euros plus bike hire. Another good supplier is Bike Point (www.bikepointtenerife.com), with locations in El Médano and Playa de las Américas.

Paragliding, windsurfing, hiking –
if you love the outdoor life, there's
sure to be something here for you

CLIMBING

At *Forestal Park Tenerife (El Rosario |
www.forestalpark.com)*, a ropes course
in a pine forest, you can put your abil-
ities to the test. Zip-lines up to 200 m
(660 ft) long and platforms 30 m (100
ft) up in the air will give you a real rush.
Admission 22 euros

DIVING

Diving schools offer courses and also trips
to some truly amazing underwater sites
– not too far from the coast. Snorkelers
exploring the inshore waters will catch a
glimpse of a few small fish, but accompa-
nied scuba divers will be able to see bar-
racudas, parrot fish, mantas, tuna and,
if they're lucky, even whales and dolphins. The *Centro de Buceo Atlantik diving
school (tel. 9 22 36 28 01 | tenerife-buceo.
com)* in Puerto de la Cruz runs dives from
38 euros, courses for beginners starting at 75. In Playa de las Américas, the
Aqua-Marina Dive Centre (Local 249-A |

C.C. Compostela Beach | tel. 9 22 79 79 44 | www.aquamarinadivingtenerife.com) is highly recommended. In *Playa Paraíso,* the *Dive Center Aquanautic (tel. 9 22 74 18 81 | www.tauchen-auf-teneriffa. com)* offers a large selection of tours. The same can be said for the *Divería diving centre (Plaza 12 | tel. 6 03 76 27 54 | www. diveria.net)* in Alcalá.

GOLF

Golfers can putt and tee off from three 27-hole, four 18-hole and two 9-hole golf courses throughout the year. Anyone can use them upon payment of the green fee (details can be found under Sports & Leisure in the various regional chapters).

HIKING

Tenerife is a paradise for everyone who likes to explore the landscape on foot. The most beautiful hiking areas include the *Valle de la Orotava,* the A*naga Mountains* and the *Parque Nacional del Teide.* And in the south, there is the enticing *Barranco del Infierno.* Most of the trails are well signposted, but due to the often enormous differences in elevation, it's advisable to make sure you're in good physical shape before you set off. Good preparation, sufficient provisions and caution are all important. An up-to-date hiking guide is also advisable. Inexperienced hikers may wish to join a tour led by an experienced guide. Several agencies in the holiday resorts offer guided hikes at different levels of difficulty, such as *www.digasports.co.uk*

PARAGLIDING

There are no fewer than 40 different take-off points on the island. The best one, *Izaña,* lies on the *Cumbre Dorsal* at a height of 2,350 m (7,710 ft) behind the observatory. Tandem and solo flights, equipment hire and courses are offered by *Tenerfly (C/ Reykjavik | Adeje | tel. 6 37 55 92 22 | www.tenerfly.com). Flights from 90 euros*

RIDING

There is a riding stable at the *Amarilla Golf & Country Club* near *Los Abrigos.* Several fincas specialise in riding holidays. The *Finca Estrella (Fuente de Vega 24 | tel. 9 22 81 43 82 | www.teneriffa-reiten. com/text/english)* near *Icod de los Vinos* offers hacks in the still unspoilt woodland nearby.

SURFING

Surfers will find excellent opportunities on the north coast, however, the best place on the island is *Playa de Benijo* behind the Anaga Mountains, but the journey there can take a long time. A good spot for beginners is the *Playa de Martiánez* in Puerto de la Cruz, but surfers wanting more challenging waves are likely to make for the *Playa del Socorro* or the *Playa Punta Brava* west of Puerto de la Cruz. The conditions are also ideal off *El Médano* in the south.

SPAS

Since as early as the 19th century, visitors have been coming to Tenerife to restore the health. Of course, their good old thermal spas of the 19th century are passé. Nowadays, spas are meant to help you relax both physically and mentally. Most four- and five-star hotels offer attractive spas that non-resident guests can also use for a fee.

Puerto de la Cruz is home to the impressive *Oriental Spa Garden* in the hotel *Botánico (hotelbotanico.com)* and its slightly smaller neighbour spa at the *Bahía Príncipe San Felipe (www.bahia-principe.com)*. At the *Hotel Océano (www.oceano-tenerife.com)* in Punta del Hidalgo also employs a team of doctors and therapists to provide first-class treatment. In the south of the island is the traditional *Mare Nostrum Spa (www.marenostrumspa.es)* in Playa de las Américas while close by is the highly recommended *Aqua Club Termal (www.aquaclubtermal.com)* – the only independently operated thermal baths on the island. An exclusive ambience can be en-

the green landscape around.

WINDSURFING

The hot spots are mainly along the southeast coast – with wind strengths in winter usually around 5, in summer as high as 8, experienced windsurfers love it here. *El Cabezo* and *La Jaquita* (wind strengths 4–8) are recommended only for experts; every year world championship events are staged in the inshore waters near *El Médano* (wind strengths 3–5).
The *Surf Center (C/ La Gaviota | tel. 9 22 17 66 88 | www.surfcenter.el-medano.*

Surfing the Atlantic waves is never easy

joyed in the *Thai Zen SPAce* in the *Hotel El Mirador (www.elmiradorgranhotel.com)* at the Bahía del Duque as well as in the spa belonging to the *Sheraton La Caleta (www.sheratonlacaleta.com)*. Elegantly furnished with wooden features is the *Abama-Hotel* spa *(www.abamahotelresort.com)* with a view of

com) wind and kitesurfing courses for all levels of ability. It, of course, includes board hire and a safe place to store your own boards. If you feel like giving windsurfing a try, the more sheltered conditions off *Playa de las Américas* and along the west coast are much more favourable for novices.

TRAVEL WITH KIDS

Little guests are important guests. The main resort hotels have kids' pools, play areas, sometimes supervised, sometimes with entertainers (check when booking). Los Cristianos and Los Gigantes both boast beaches that are perfect for children.

In many places, on 5 January, the day before Epiphany – *Los Reyes Magos* – there are INSIDERTIP children's parades, likewise during Carnaval (ask at the tourist office for information).

THE NORTHWEST

CAMELLO CENTER (141 D2) (*D5*)

6 km (4 miles) uphill from Garaicho, dromedaries and camels can be used for rides through the volcanic landscape. It's a shame that the trip only lasts 20 minutes. But there are also goats, ponies and donkeys to look at, and if you're hungry, you can order a Canarian lunch menu. If a tour bus has just arrived, the waiting times can be long. *Daily 10am–5pm | admission 10 euros, children (aged 3–12) 5 euros | El Tanque | TF-82, km 10.2 | tel. 9 22 13 61 91 | www.camellocenter.es*

LAGO DE MARTIÁNEZ ●
(136 C5) (*H4*)

Puerto de la Cruz is by far the most popular resort on Tenerife's north coast, but it doesn't have many beaches. Also, as the Atlantic Ocean can unleash some powerful forces against the *playas*, children cannot swim safely here.

César Manrique, the brilliant architect

Parrots in the park, fun in the water and hands-on science – varied entertainment is guaranteed

and landscape architect from Lanzarote, came up with a solution. In 1977 he designed the Promenade Lido San Telmo and the Lago de Martiánez, a landscaped aquatic park situated on different levels in the cliffs consisting of several large saltwater pools, a large lake with islands of lava rock, waterfalls, fountains, cafeterias, a restaurant and lush greenery. For children there are climbing frames, a bright red, walk-in grotto area and they just love the warm jacuzzi pool. Suitable for children from eight years of age. *Daily 10am–5pm | admission 5.50, euros, children up to 10 pay 2.50 euros | Costa Martiánez*

LORO PARQUE ★ (136 B5) *(𝄞 G–H4)*
This vast zoo is situated at the end of Playa Jardín and consists of parks, tropical gardens, animal enclosures, aquariums and arenas for (animal) shows and special events. The park keeps the world's largest collection of parrots in one place; among the approx. 350 species and 4,000 animals are

some very rare specimens threatened by extinction. Some of them are even bred at Loro Parque.

For many years the park has kept other animals – from crocodiles and gorillas to white Bengal tigers. A panoramic cinema shows how a bird views the world. But even better is the "Katandra": a huge outdoor aviary, where visitors big and small can climb up ladders and suspension bridges to the tree-tops to see a wide range of exotic feathered friends visitors and in an underwater tunnel, sharks and manta rays can be observed from just a few centimetres away. The orcas are another major attraction. The giant black-and-white killer whales put on shows in their huge pool. Even though it may delight (tiny) spectators, it's a thorn in the side for animal-rights activists. They argue that no matter how big the pool is, it will always be too small for animals that swim thousands of kilometres in the ocean. This criticism

Thai feeling on Tenerife: surfing the waves in the Siam Park

at close quarters.

Some 200 creatures, notably king and rockhopper penguins, live in the world's largest penguinarium at temperatures around freezing point. It's all beneath a huge dome, from which a constant shower of man-made snow descends.

Some 20,000 fish frolic in a huge Perspex cylinder. Dolphin and sea lion shows are staged to entertain the essentially applies to all animals in captivity and aims for the abolition of zoos... *Daily 8:30am–6:45pm (last entry) | admission 34 euros, children (4–11) 23 euros, discount on second visit; combined ticket with Siam Park 58 and 39.50 euros respectively | Playa Punta Brava (free mini-train every 20 mins from Playa de Martiánez) | www. loroparque.com*

THE NORTHEAST

MUSEO DE LA CIENCIA Y EL COSMOS
(138 B3) (*M3*)
Interactive displays and easy-to-understand examples in this Science Museum in La Laguna help children from about eight years of age to learn through play about the universe, the earth and man. Most exhibits with explanations in English. *Tue–Sun 9am–7pm | admission 5 euros | Av. de los Menceyes 70 | www.museosdetenerife.org*

PARQUE MARÍTIMO CÉSAR MANRIQUE (138 C4) (*N3*)
The open-air water park in Santa Cruz is fun for kids with several several swimming pools, islands of volcanic rock and large open areas for sunbathing. It was designed by the artist César Manrique. Small cafeterias serve drinks and snacks. *Mon–Fri 10am–5pm, Sat/Sun 10am–8pm | admission 3 euros, children 1.50 euros | Av. de la Constitución 5*

THE SOUTHWEST

AQUALAND (144 C4) (*E4*)
A saltwater theme park with pools, water slides and flumes, waterfalls and a lazy river, so you can drift gently through the whole complex. Dolphinarium with daily shows, play areas. Plus snack bars and shops. You will have to pay extra for loungers, etc. and shows. *Daily 10am–5pm | admission 21.50 euros, children (3–4 years) 7 euros, (5–10) 15,50 euros | San Eugenio Alto | Autopista del Sur, exit 29 | www.aqualand.es/tenerife*

ÁGUILAS JUNGLE PARK
(145 D4) (*E11*)
A jungle on Tenerife? 7 ha (17 acres) of exotic vegetation, lakes and waterfalls are located above the resort. Watch eagles, vultures, falcons, owls and other raptors at feeding time and also on the hunt for prey. You can also marvel at white tigers, lions, penguins, hippos, crocodiles and orang-utans. And then there are cafeterias, a cactus garden, climbing frames and pedalos on a minilake. *Daily 10am–5:30pm | admission 26 euros, children under 1.40 m (4'7") pay less | directions: Ctra. Los Cristianos–Arona, km 3 (TF-1, junction 27) | free buses from the resorts in the south | www.aguilasjunglepark.com*

SIAM PARK ★ (144 C5) (*E11*)
Inspired by the architecture of Thailand, Siam Park's theme is the "Kingdom of the Water". Extending over an area of 14 ha (34 acres), there are temples, giant dragons and a market on stilts, as well as eight waterslides, one more exciting than the other – for example whooshing through a shark tank. Surging waves 3 m (10 ft) high reach a man-made bay with a white sandy beach. Younger children will love the "Lost City", an adventure playground in water where there are hissing and gurgling sound everywhere. The highlight is a hollow giant's head that fills with water. Once it has filled up, it tilts over, its contents plummeting in a powerful waterfall. Very crowded in the summer. *Daily 10am–5pm | admission 34 euros, children 23 euros, combined ticket with Loro Parque 58 and 39.50 euros respectively | Autopista del Sur, exit 28 | www.siampark.net*

FESTIVALS & EVENTS

Practically every day of the year somewhere on Tenerife, there will be a procession or the commemoration of a saint. But there is good reason for this, as the island has always been pitilessly exposed to the forces of nature, whether sea or volcano. Each village has its own patron saint.

Easter and Corpus Christi take a form of pilgrimages. At farmers' festivals and other traditional events a parade of beautifully decorated ox carts usually get things off to a colourful start. Then the partying gets going with dancing and feasting. Music and ballet evenings in Santa Cruz, rock and folk festivals in La Laguna demonstrate that the island is very much part of mainstream European culture. And the annual Carnaval has to be the wildest north of Rio.

FESTIVALS & EVENTS

JANUARY/FEBRUARY

For a whole month, Santa Cruz de Tenerife hosts the *Festival de Música de Canarias*, where music from all over the world, from chamber music to philharmonic concerts, is performed in the Teatro Guimerá or in the Auditorio. *www.festivaldecanarias.com*

FEBRUARY/MARCH

Wild celebrations in the weeks before Lent for the ★ *Carnaval (www.carnavaltenerife.com)*. It culminates in processions and dance festivals in Santa Cruz de Tenerife.

MARCH/APRIL

Magnificent *processions* take place during the whole of Easter week, especially in the religious centre of La Laguna. The climax is a series of doleful processions on Good Friday.

MAY

Fiesta de San Isidro: Celebrations take place around the 15 May in honour of the patron saint of farmers: in Granadilla, Los Realejos and La Orotava. The *Tinerfeños* dress up in traditional costume, play music and dance.

MAY/JUNE

More processions to mark ★ *Corpus Christi* – the best ones are in La Laguna and La Orotava. Magnificent flower carpets and coloured volcanic sand are laid out on the streets and squares.

JULY

On the second Sunday the *Fiesta y Romería del San Benito Abad* is celebrated with a pilgrimage and grand fair to honour the patron saint of La Laguna.

Nuestra Señora del Carmen, the patron saint of fishermen, is remembered on 16 July with picturesque processions of boats in Santa Cruz de Tenerife and Puerto de la Cruz.

25 July is *St James's Day* and another occasion for a party in many towns.

AUGUST

INSIDER TIP *Romería de la Virgen de Candelaria*: On 15 August tens of thousands of pilgrims make their way to Candelaria to pay homage to the island's patron saint.

On the next day the people of Garachico let their hair down for the *Romería de San Roque*, a classic farmer's festival with lively processions. Also in the outlying communities.

SEPTEMBER

As part of the *Fiestas del Cristo* the best folk music bands in the Canaries gather in La Laguna for the two-day INSIDER TIP *Festival Sabandeño*, an event visited by thousands of young people.

NOVEMBER

In all odd-numbered years the island stages *Festival Foto-Noviembre*, a forum for internationally-renowned photographers to display their work. The main centres are Santa Cruz and La Laguna. *www.fotonoviembre.com*

NATIONAL HOLIDAYS

1 Jan	New Year's Day
6 Jan	Epiphany
19 March	*San José* (St Joseph's Day)
March/April	Good Friday
1 May	Labour Day
30 May	*Día de las Islas Canarias* (Canary Islands Day)
May/June	Corpus Christi
25 July	*Santiago Apóstol* (St James's Day)
15 Aug	Assumption
12 Oct	*Día de la Hispanidad* (Columbus Day)
1 Nov	All Saints' Day
6 Dec	*Día de la Constitución* (Constitution Day)
8 Dec	Immaculate Conception
25 Dec	Christmas

TRAVEL TIPS

ARRIVAL

✈ Cheap flights are available from the UK and Ireland with Ryanair, easyJet and Thomas Cook (UK flight time from approx. 4 hours). Flights with no hotel booking cost between 300 and 500 euros. Scheduled flights are much more expensive and nearly always involve a stopover. There are no direct flights from the USA.

There are two airports: the southern airport, *Reina Sofía,* which is served by most international airlines, is a 20-minute drive from Playa de las Américas and Los Cristianos and about 1 hour from Puerto de la Cruz.

Scheduled buses run from the South Airport to Playa de las Américas (nos. 111, 343, 350; approx. 3 euros), Santa Cruz de Tenerife (no. 711; approx. 8 euros) and Puerto de la Cruz (no. 343; approx. 12 euros).

All national scheduled flights and many low-cost airlines land at *Tenerife Norte*

RESPONSIBLE TRAVEL

It doesn't take a lot to be environmentally friendly whilst travelling. Don't just think about your carbon footprint whilst flying to and from your holiday destination but also about how you can protect nature and culture abroad. As a tourist it is especially important to respect nature, look out for local products, cycle instead of driving, save water and much more. If you would like to find out more about eco-tourism please visit: *www.ecotourism.org*

airport near La Laguna. For flight information call *9 22 63 59 99.* Inter-Canary Island flights depart from here and also from *Reina Sofía (Information tel. 9 22 39 20 37).*

🚢 Once a week at 5pm a car ferry operated by Compañía Trasmediterránea-Acciona leaves from the southern Spanish port of Cádiz. The crossing to Santa Cruz de Tenerife takes 31 hours (return trip also once a week). A fare for a single journey starts from 200 euros per person (in a 4-bed cabin). A car costs roughly the same. Booking through travel agencies or at www.trasmediterranea.es.

BUSES & TRAM

Buses on Tenerife are called *guaguas* (pronounced guahuah). Santa Cruz's central bus station, *Estación de Guaguas*, is at Avenida 3 de Mayo 47. Green TITSA buses run from here to almost every town on Tenerife. Nos. 103 and 110 are express buses. You can buy a *Bono* ticket at bus stations in Santa Cruz and other holiday resorts. This gives holders a 10 per cent (or more) reduction on all fares. *Information is available in Spanish and English on 9 22 53 13 00 Mon–Fri 7am–9pm* and also on the internet at *www.titsa.com.* The Tram No. 1 *(tranvía)* runs every 5–15 minutes between Santa Cruz and the university town of La Laguna – the Bono Ticket is also valid here *(www.metrotenerife.com).*

CAMPING

Wild camping is not allowed on Tenerife. It has several campsites, e.g. *Camping-Caravaning Nauta (Cañada Blanca |*

Ctra 6225, km 1.5 | Las Galletas | Arona | tel. 9 22 78 51 18 | www.campingnauta.com); Camping El Castillo de Himeche (Guía de Isora | mobile tel. 6 86 25 89 54 | www.campingelcastillodehimeche.com); Camping Playa de la Arena (Taraconte | tel. 6 69 81 15 35).

Free use of the public campsites in the mountains, some of which are in very attractive spots (with or without sanitary facilities) is allowed with the prior permission of the *Oficina de Medio Ambiente (Av. de Anaga 35 | Santa Cruz | tel. 92 24 75 95)*. If you have a caravan, it is permitted to spend at least one night on public carparks or on the street, in remote spots longer.

CAR HIRE

Car rental companies run offices in the airports, in all the holiday resorts and also in many hotels. The hire charges for a small car could well be less than 25 euros per day (including taxes and fully comprehensive insurance). *Cicar (tel. 9 28 82 29 00 | www.cicar.com)* is a reliable local company, which has bureaux in all airports, ports and holiday resorts. The cars are well maintained, and in the event of a breakdown roadside assistance arrives promptly. Rental cars must have a high-visibility vest on board. All-terrain vehicles, trikes and motorcycles, which you can also rent everywhere, are considerably more expensive.

CLIMATE & WHEN TO GO

Tenerife's mild climate means only small fluctuations in temperature. In the arid south, even in winter, temperatures hardly ever fall below 18 °C and only rarely rise above 24 °C. In summer, however, the temperature can stay at 30 °C and above for weeks. Even at moderate altitudes weak air currents can give rise to an oppressive heat. The temperatures in the north are often significantly lower than in the south. At over 500 m (1,640 ft) above sea level in winter it can be qui-

BUDGETING

Taxis	1.78 £ / from 2.68 £	per km / basic pickup charge
Coffee	from 1.78 £	for a cup of coffee
Souvenir	1.34 £	for one trelitzia plant
Wine	from 1.78 £	for a glass (0.2l)
Petrol	just over 0,89 £	for 1 l of unleaded
Tapa	from 2.14 £	for a small snack

te cold. So remember to pack not just a hat and a sweater, but also a cagoule. As water temperatures in Tenerife are always in the 18 ° to 24 °C range, it's fine to swim in the sea any day of the year. The best time to visit the island is from November to March.

CONSULATES & EMBASSIES

UK CONSULATE
Mon–Fri 8:30am–1:30pm | Plaza Weyler, 8, 1° | 38003 Santa Cruz de Tenerife | tel. 928 26 25 08

US CONSULATE

Edificio ARCA | C/ Los Martínez Escobar, 3, Oficina 7 | 35007 Las Palmas | tel. 928 27 12 59

CUSTOMS

Although Spain is in the EU, there are restrictions when returning to the UK and the USA from the Canary Islands for anyone over 17 years of age. Maximum amounts are 200 cigarettes or 50 cigars or 250 grams of tobacco, 1 litre of spirits, 2 litres of wine, 50 g of perfume, 250 cl of Eau de Cologne.

DRIVING

The roads on Tenerife are good and safe. Maximum speed: in urban areas 50 km/h (30 mph), on country roads 90 km/h (56 mph) and on motorways 120 km/h (75 mph) The breath-alcohol limit is 0.025%, which roughly corresponds to a blood-alcohol limit of 0.05%. Drivers must also keep a high-visibility jacket in the car. Telephone calls may only be made using hands-free mobile phones.

Parking is not allowed where there are yellow markings by the kerb; a parking fee is payable where there are blue lines. Only *grúas*, licensed companies, are permitted to tow away vehicles.

EMERGENCY

There is one number for all emergencies: *112*.

HEALTH

The greatest risk for tourists is high exposure to the sun (even in winter). So sunburnt skin, particularly at the start of the holiday, is a frequent, but avoidable occurrence. A sunscreen with high sun protection factor (from 20) should therefore be applied every day – not only on the beach, but also when hiking. Some form of head wear is also important.

PUERTO STREET ART

An appealing sight? Giant graffiti in a pensioners' paradise? Tourists sit down in a terrace restaurant in the culinary street El Lomo in Puerto de la Cruz, and what do they see? A huge painting full of insects spanning six stories! Cockroaches, stag beetles and millipedes intertwined and stacked up on top of each other reach from the ground towards the sky. This mega graffiti was created by the award-winning Belgian artist Roa, who has made paintings all over the world of often injured animals typical of each place. The graffiti "The Frontier of Paradise" by Víctor Ash at Calle Méquinez 4 also has a local connection: a wire-mesh fence made of human bodies blocks access to palm trees and the sea and recalls the Africans travelling from the neighbouring continent to the Canaries in nutshell rafts. Many more gigantic paintings are spread through the historic fishing quarter La Ranilla.

DOCTORS & HOSPITALS

If you have a European Health Insurance Card (EHIC), you will be treated free of charge by doctors, outpatient clinics and hospitals, which are part of the Spanish Seguridad Social system. Otherwise, you should request a detailed invoice *(factura)*, so that you can claim a refund from your holiday insurance company.

Santa Cruz de Tenerife: *Hospital Nuestra Señora de la Candelaria (24-hour service | Ctra. Rosario 145 | Tel. 60 9 22 20 00). Hospiten Rambla (La Rambla 115 | tel. 9 22 29 16 00 | www.hospiten.es).*

Playa de las Américas/Los Cristianos: *Espacio de Salud DKV (Mon–Fri 8am–8pm, 24-hour service | Av. Gómez Cuesta 22 | Playa de las Américas | tel. 9 22 10 22 02).*

Hospiten Sur *(24-hour service and hotel visits | C/ Siete Islas 8 | tel. 9 22 75 00 22 | www.hospiten.es).*

Puerto de la Cruz: *Salus Medical Centre (24-hour service | Av. Betancourt y Molina 20 A | tel. 9 22 38 06 51).*

PHARMACIES

Pharmacies *(farmacias)* are recognisable by the green Maltese cross *(Mon–Fri 9am–1pm and 4pm–7pm, Sat 9am–1pm).* The sign *Farmacia de Guardia* will give the address of the nearest duty pharmacy.

INFORMATION BEFORE YOU GO

SPANISH NATIONAL TOURISM OFFICES

Tourist information is available from the Spanish tourism offices and also at *www. spain.info*

- 6th Floor 64 North Row | London W1K 7DE | info.londres@tourspain.es
– 1395 Brickell Avenue, Suite 1130 | Miami, FL 33131 | oetmiami@tourspain.es
– 845 North Michigan Av, Suite 915-E | Chicago, IL 60611 | chicago@tourspain.es
– 8383 Wilshire Blvd., Suite 956 | Beverly Hills, CA 90211 | losangeles@tourspain.es
– 60 East 42nd Street, Suite 5300 (53rd Floor) | New York, NY 10165-0039 | nuevayork@tourspain.es

INFORMATION ON TENERIFE

In the arrivals hall of *Reina Sofía Airport (Arrivals hall; Mon–Fri 9am–9pm | Sat 9am–5pm | tel. 9 22 39 20 37).* Other information points in all larger resorts.

INTERNET & WIFI

Now hotels in all categories offer WiFi hotspots. However, these are often not included in the room charge and so must be paid for sometimes at expensive rates (e.g. 10 mins for 1 euro).

If you don't have your laptop or smartphone with you, you may be able to make use of the hotel's internet computer, but again a charge may be payable. A slightly cheaper alternative is an internet café. There will usually be one in the shopping centres in larger resorts. *Salones recreativos,* i.e. amusement arcades, often have a few computer terminals.

NATURIST BEACHES

Naturism is normally only common on a few beaches – for example, at *Playa de la Tejita* west of the Montaña Roja near *El Médano,* at *Playa de Montaña Amarilla* (Costa del Silencio) or at *Playa de las Gaviotas* near Playa de las Teresitas.

PHONE & MOBILE PHONE

You can phone home with coins or phone cards *(teletarjeta),* available from post offices and newspaper kiosks for 6 or 12 euros. The phone box will be marked *internacional*. In many holiday resorts, there are call shops known as *locutorios*, where you pay when the call is over.

To call the UK, dial 0044, the USA 001, then the area code but without 0, followed by the subscriber's number. If you wish to phone Tenerife from abroad, the code is 0034, then dial the subscriber's number.

Using your mobile phone will not pose any problems. As of June 2017, roaming charges no longer apply within the EU. Making calls to other EU countries should normally not cost more than at home.

OPENING TIMES

Restaurants are usually open between 1pm–4pm and 7pm–11pm and in holiday resorts from 12pm until nightfall or even later. Bars and restaurants often close on Sundays at 3pm! Many businesses take a siesta (1pm–5pm) while shopping centres normally stay open all day from 10am–8pm or even later.

POST

On most of the island post offices *(correos)*, where you also buy your stamps *(sellos)*, are open Mon–Fri 8:30am–2:30pm, but in Santa Cruz de Tenerife and Puerto de la Cruz they stay open until 8:30pm and are also open on Saturday morning. Official letter boxes are yellow and are only for letters marked with stamps from the state postal service.

PRICES

The price you will have to pay for services

WEATHER ON TENERIFE

	Jan	Feb	March	April	May	June	July	Aug	Sept	Oct	Nov	Dec
Daytime temperatures in °C/°F	21/70	21/70	22/72	23/73	24/75	26/79	28/82	29/84	28/82	26/79	23/73	22/72
Nighttime temperatures in °C/°F	14/57	14/57	15/59	16/61	17/63	19/66	21/70	21/70	21/70	19/66	17/63	16/61
☀	5	6	7	8	10	11	11	11	9	7	5	5
☂	7	5	3	2	1	0	0	0	1	4	6	7
≈	19/66	18/64	18/64	18/64	19/66	20/68	21/70	22/72	23/73	23/73	21/70	20/68

(e.g. car repairs) is likely to be slightly higher than in the UK or in the US. Food costs about the same.

RURAL TOURISM

If you go on holiday to Tenerife, you don't have to stay in a hotel or villa complex. There are a number of agencies which rent out more than 50 accommodations in the country, ranging from fincas for 10 persons to a cave. They have usually been fully renovated and are equipped with modern facilities. Prices are generally much lower than in tourist hotels.

The main agency is *Attur (Asociación Tinerfeña de Turismo Rural | Mon–Fri 9am–2pm | C/ Méndez Núñez 17 | Santa Cruz de Tenerife | tel. 9 02 21 55 82 | www.attur.es)* with over 30 properties.

SMOKING

In 2011, Spain adopted the strongest anti-smoking laws in the EU. Proprietors risk draconian fines if customers smoke in enclosed public places, i.e. in all restaurants, bars and cafés. Separate smoking rooms are not permissible either. Even smoking outdoors is restricted; for example, smoking a cigarette in close proximity to a children's playground is an offence.

TAXIS

All taxis are licensed and equipped with a meter, which must be turned on before each trip. The fare will be based on 2 euros per kilometre plus a basic pick-up charge (approx. 3 euros) and surcharges for Sundays and public holidays, night-time fares, journeys to the port and to the airport and also for large items of luggage. If you would like to make an island tour by taxi, make sure you agree on the price beforehand.

TIME

Unlike mainland Spain, Tenerife runs on Greenwich Mean Time, so visitors from the UK and Ireland DO NOT need to adjust their watches.

IMMIGRATION

Citizens of the UK & Ireland, USA, Canada, Australia and New Zealand need only a valid passport to enter all countries of the EU. Children below the age of 12 need a children's passport. Check online for the latest travel advice and entry requirements: www.gov.uk/foreign-travel-advice (UK Citizens) or www.state.gov/travel (US Citizens)

CURRENCY CONVERTER

£	€	€	£
1	1.40	1	0.72
3	4.17	3	2.15
5	6.96	5	3.59
13	18.08	13	9.34
40	55.65	40	28.75
75	104	75	53.89
120	167	120	86
250	348	250	180
500	696	500	359

$	€	€	$
1	0.92	1	1.09
3	2.75	3	3.27
5	4.58	5	5.45
13	11.92	13	14.18
40	36.67	40	43.64
75	69	75	81.82
120	110	120	131
250	229	250	273
500	458	500	545

For current exchange rates see www.xe.com

USEFUL PHRASES SPANISH

PRONUNCIATION

c	before 'e' and 'i' like 'th' in 'thin'
ch	as in English
g	before 'e' and 'i' like the 'ch' in Scottish 'loch'
gue, gui/que, qui	like 'get', 'give', the 'u' is not spoken, i.e. 'ke', 'ki'
j	always like the 'ch' in Scottish 'loch'
ll, y	like 'lli' in 'million'; some speak it like 'y' in 'yet'
ñ	"nj"
z	like "th" in "thin"

IN BRIEF

Yes/No/Maybe	sí/no/quizás
Please/Thank you	por favor/gracias
Hello!/Goodbye!/See you	¡Hola!/¡Adiós!/¡Hasta luego!
Good morning!/afternoon!/evening!/night!	¡Buenos días!/¡Buenos días!/¡Buenas tardes!/¡Buenas noches!
Excuse me, please!	¡Perdona!/¡Perdone!
May I...?/Pardon?	¿Puedo...?/¿Cómo dice?
My name is...	Me llamo...
What's your name?	¿Cómo se llama usted?/¿Cómo te llamas?
I'm from...	Soy de...
I would like to .../Have you got ...?	Querría.../¿Tiene usted...?
How much is...?	¿Cuánto cuesta...?
I (don't) like that	Esto (no) me gusta.
good/bad/broken/doesn't work	bien/mal/roto/no funciona
too much/much/little/all/nothing	demasiado/mucho/poco/todo/nada
Help!/Attention!/Caution!	¡Socorro!/¡Atención!/¡Cuidado!
ambulance/police/fire brigade	ambulancia/policía/bomberos
May I take a photo here	¿Podría fotografiar aquí?

DATE & TIME

Monday/Tuesday/Wednesday	lunes/martes/miércoles
Thursday/Friday/Saturday	jueves/viernes/sábado
Sunday/working day/holiday	domingo/laborable/festivo

¿Hablas español?

"Do you speak Spanish?" This guide will help you to
say the basic words and phrases in Spanish.

today/tomorrow/yesterday	hoy/mañana/ayer
hour/minute/second/moment	hora/minuto/segundo/momento
day/night/week/month/year	día/noche/semana/mes/año
now/immediately/before/after	ahora/enseguida/antes/después
What time is it?	¿Qué hora es?
It's three o'clock/It's half past three	Son las tres/Son las tres y media
a quarter to four/a quarter past four	cuatro menos cuarto/ cuatro y cuarto

TRAVEL

open/closed/opening times	abierto/cerrado/horario
entrance/exit	entrada/acceso salida
departure/arrival	salida/llegada
toilets/ladies/gentlemen	aseos/señoras/caballeros
free/occupied	libre/ocupado
(not) drinking water	agua (no) potable
Where is...?/Where are...?	¿Dónde está...?/¿Dónde están...?
left/right	izquierda/derecha
straight ahead/back	recto/atrás
close/far	cerca/lejos
traffic lights/corner/crossing	semáforo/esquina/cruce
bus/tram/Underground/taxi/cab	guagua/tranvía/metro/taxi
bus stop/cab stand	parada/parada de taxis
parking lot/parking garage	parking/garaje
street map/map	plano de la ciudad/mapa
train station/harbour/airport	estación/puerto/aeropuerto
ferry/quay	transbordador/muelle
schedule/ticket/supplement	horario/billete/suplemento
single/return	sencillo/ida y vuelta
train/track/platform	tren/vía/andén
delay/strike	retraso/huelga
I would like to rent...	Querría alquilar...
a car/a bicycle/a boat	un coche/una bicicleta/un barco
petrol/gas station	gasolinera
petrol/gas / diesel	gasolina/diesel
breakdown/repair shop	avería/taller

FOOD & DRINK

Could you please book a table for tonight for four?	Resérvenos, por favor, una mesa para cuatro personas para hoy por la noche.
on the terrace/by the window	en la terraza/junto a la ventana

The menu, please.	¡El menú, por favor!
Could I please have...?	¿Podría traerme...por favor?
bottle/carafe/glass	botella/jarra/vaso
knife/fork/spoon	cuchillo/tenedor/cuchara
salt/pepper/sugar	sal/pimienta/azúcar
vinegar/oil/milk/cream/lemon	vinagre/aceite/leche/limón
cold/too salty/not cooked	frío/demasiado salado/sin hacer
with/without ice/sparkling	con/sin hielo/gas
vegetarian/allergy	vegetariano/vegetariana/alergía
May I have the bill, please?	Querría pagar, por favor.
bill/receipt/tip	cuenta/recibo/propina

SHOPPING

pharmacy/chemist	farmacia/droguería
baker/market	panadería/mercado
butcher/fishmonger	carnicería/pescadería
shopping centre/department store	centro comercial/grandes almacenes
shop/supermarket/kiosk	tienda/supermercado/quiosco
100 grammes/1 kilo	cien gramos/un kilo
expensive/cheap/price/more/less	caro/barato/precio/más/menos
organically grown	de cultivo ecológico

ACCOMMODATION

I have booked a room	He reservado una habitación.
Do you have any...left?	¿Tiene todavía...?
single room/double room	habitación individual/habitación doble
breakfast/half board/	desayuno/media pensión/
full board (American plan)	pensión completa
at the front/seafront/garden view	hacia delante/hacia el mar/hacia el jardín
shower/sit-down bath	ducha/baño
balcony/terrace	balcón/terraza
key/room card	llave/tarjeta
luggage/suitcase/bag	equipaje/maleta/bolso
swimming pool/spa/sauna	piscina/spa/sauna
soap/toilet paper/nappy (diaper)	jabón/papel higiénico/pañal
cot/high chair/nappy changing	cuna/trona/cambiar los pañales
deposit	anticipo/caución

BANKS, MONEY & CREDIT CARDS

bank/ATM/	banco/cajero automático/
pin code	número secreto
cash/credit card	en efectivo/tarjeta de crédito
bill/coin/change	billete/moneda/cambio

USEFUL PHRASES

HEALTH

doctor/dentist/paediatrician	médico/dentista/pediatra
hospital/emergency clinic	hospital/urgencias
fever/pain/inflamed/injured	fiebre/dolor/inflamado/herido
diarrhoea/nausea/sunburn	diarrea/náusea/quemadura de sol
plaster/bandage/ointment/cream	tirita/vendaje/pomada/crema
pain reliever/tablet/suppository	calmante/comprimido/supositorio

POST, TELECOMMUNICATIONS & MEDIA

stamp/letter/postcard	sello/carta/postal
I need a landline phone card/	Necesito una tarjeta telefónica/
I'm looking for a prepaid card for my mobile	Busco una tarjeta prepago para mi móvil
Where can I find internet access?	¿Dónde encuentro un acceso a internet?
dial/connection/engaged	marcar/conexión/ocupado
socket/adapter/charger	enchufe/adaptador/cargador
computer/battery/	ordenador/batería/
rechargeable battery	batería recargable
e-mail address/at sign (@)	(dirección de) correo electrónico/arroba
internet address (URL)	dirección de internet
internet connection/wifi	conexión a internet/wifi
e-mail/file/print	archivo/imprimir

LEISURE, SPORTS & BEACH

beach/sunshade/lounger	playa/sombrilla/tumbona
low tide/high tide/current	marea baja/marea alta/corriente
funicular/chairlift	funicular/telesilla

NUMBERS

0	cero	14	catorce
1	un, uno, una	15	quince
2	dos	16	dieciséis
3	tres	17	diecisiete
4	cuatro	18	dieciocho
5	cinco	19	diecinueve
6	seis	20	veinte
7	siete	100	cien, ciento
8	ocho	200	doscientos, doscientas
9	nueve	1000	mil
10	diez	2000	dos mil
11	once	10 000	diez mil
12	doce	1/2	medio
13	trece	1/4	un cuarto

ROAD ATLAS

The green line indicates the Discovery Tour "Tenerife at a glance"
The blue line indicates the other Discovery Tours

All tours are also marked on the pull-out map

Photo: Playa de las Teresitas

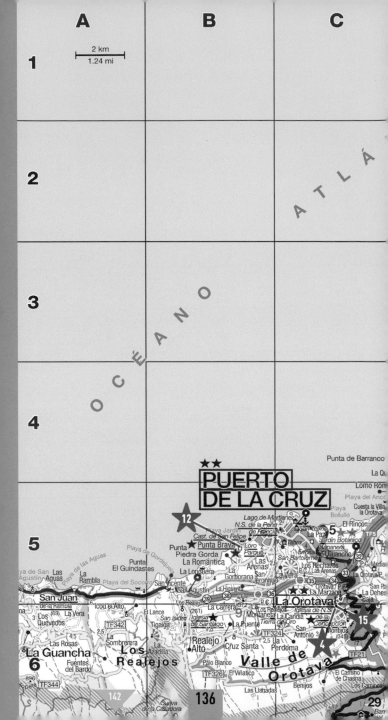

Map labels

Column D:

ICO

Punta del Viento

Mesa del Mar
Punta de la Mesa
Casas del Marqués
San José
Playa del Camello
Bahía de la Garañona
Guayonje

★Tacoronte
El Caloario (447)
Santa Catalina
★El Sauzal
San Nicolás
Punta del Puertito
Ermita de San Simón
El Cangrejillo

Punta Pesquero Alto
La Matanza

Caleta Salvaje
Punta de Juan Blas
El Caletón
Ermita de San Diego
La Breña
Punta del Sol
La Matanza (513) de Acentejo
Caleta de la Negra

Güía
El Caletón
San Antonio
La Victoria

Santa Úrsula
a Úrsula
La Vera
Los Altos Los Cercados
Tosca de Ana María
Santa Úrsula
Corujera

Ovejas
1253

la
s Órganos

Mirador Chipeque

Montaña Ayosa
2075

Column E:

Punta del Fraile
la Barranquera

Costa de Valle de Guerra
Museo de Antropol.
Valle de Guerra
4,5
La Bonifacia
El Pris
Puerto de la Madera
Garimba
San Juan
Los Perales
La Caridad
Adelantado
Lomo Colorado
Drago
Gura
Tacoronte
Los Naranjeros
Piedras de
Las
Tacoronte
Casas Altas
Agua García
Cruz de Leandro
Las Cancelillas
Ravelo
Madre del Agua
Cueva Labrada
Montaña Cabeza de Toro 1500
Las Lagunetas
Mirador Ortuño
El Diablillo
Gaitero 1747

Bodegas de Chivisaya

Araya

Las Cuevecitas
TF247
Los Loros
Malpaís

137

Column F:

1

Playa del A
Piscinas Natura
Punta Gotera
Caleta del Arco
Milán 3 Baja
TF13
2

Lomo Rivera
La Hondura 1,5
El Pico
El Cercado 3,5
Tejina
Las Toscas
Teguest

Picacho de los Lazaros
El Socorro
Calle del Vino
654 El Infierno
Tabares El Portezuelo
Cruz Grande
Guamasa
TF156
TF154
TF152
Guamasa
del Ca
Cruz Chiquita
El Rodeo El Lazaro
Los Naranjeros 1,5
Aeropuerto Norte
Aeropuerto
Los Rodeos
(Tenerife Norte)
TFN
La Cuesta
Asomada

Ortigal de Abajo
TF24
Ortigal de Arriba
938
Carboneras
TF226
1949
TF272

Birmagen
Lomo 943
Pelado

Las Rosas
El Rosario
Preventorio Infantil
Las Raíces
Las Barreras
Casa Las Señas
Machado
Nuestra
Señora del Rosario 582 5
Barranco Hondo
Taba
22

Iguiste
Iguiste
Las Caletillas
Playa de las C
Guaya Las Arenitas
Las Caletillas/Punta Larga
Playa de las Arenas
Punta Larga
Araya/Candelaria
6
★Candelaria
Basílica de la Virgen

143

Other scattered labels:

El Valle
Carril Alto
Huerta Vicho
La Esperanza
Vista de la Huerta
1216
Mirador Pico de las Flores

Bosque de la Esperanza
Lomo Chupadero
Barranco Hondo

43

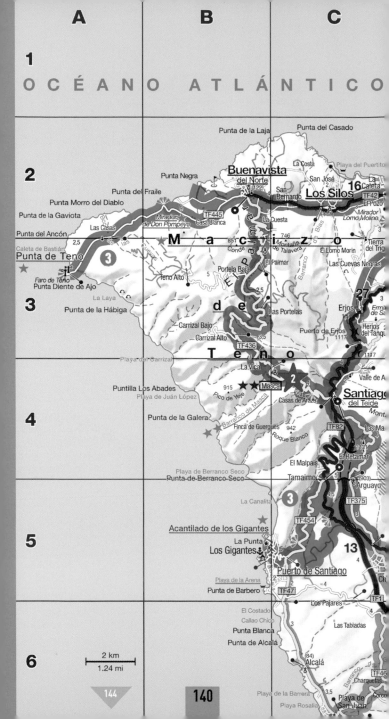

A

B

C

1

OCÉANO ATLÁNTICO

2

Punta de la Laja
Punta del Casado
La Costa
Playa del Puertito
Punta Negra
Buenavista
del Norte
San José
San Bernardo
16 La
Caleta
Los Silos
TF42
Punta del Fraile
San
Borromeo
El Pozo
Punta Morro del Diablo
TF445
Casa Blanca
La Cuesta
Mirador
Lomo Molino
Punta de la Gaviota
Mirador
de Don Pompeyo
de
Blas
Punta del Ancón
Las Casas
M a c i z o
El Lomo Morin
Tierra
del Trig
Caleta de Bastián
851
746
2.5
3
Conde
Montañe
de Talavera
Las Cuevas Negras
Punta de Teno
Faro de Teno
Teno Alto
Portela Baja
El Palmar
Punta Diente de Ajo
5
d e
Barranco
27
La Laya
2.5
Erjos
Ermi
de Si
Punta de la Hábiga
Las Portelas
Carrizal Bajo
Puerto de Erjos
Herios
del Tanqu
Carrizal Alto
T e n o
1117
TF436
3.5
1117

3

Playa del Carrizal
La Vica
Valle de A
2
Masca
Puntilla Los Abades
915
★★
Playa de Juán López
Santiago
Pico de Yeje
Casas de Araza
del Teide
Mont.
Punta de la Galera
Finca de Guergues
942
TF82
Las Ma
Roque Blanco

4

Playa de Berranco Seco
El Malpais
El Retamar
Punta-de-Berranco-Seco
Tamaimo
(1903)
Arguayo
La Canalita
3
3.5
TF375
3

5

★
TF454
Acantilado de los Gigantes
La Punta
13
Los Gigantes
Puerto de Santiago
Ch
Playa de la Arena
Punta de Barbero
TF47
Los Pajares
TF1

6

El Costado
Callao Chico
Punta Blanca
Las Tabladas
Punta de Alcalá
(84)
Alcalá
TF46
2 km
Barranco
Charquetas
1.24 mi
3.5
Coro
Playa de la Barrera
Playa de
Playa Rosalia
San Juan

144

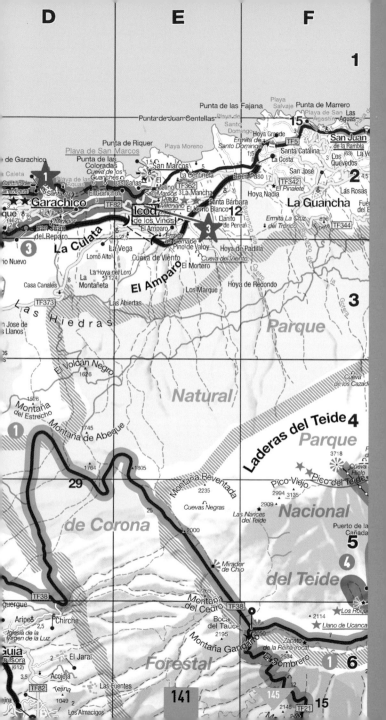

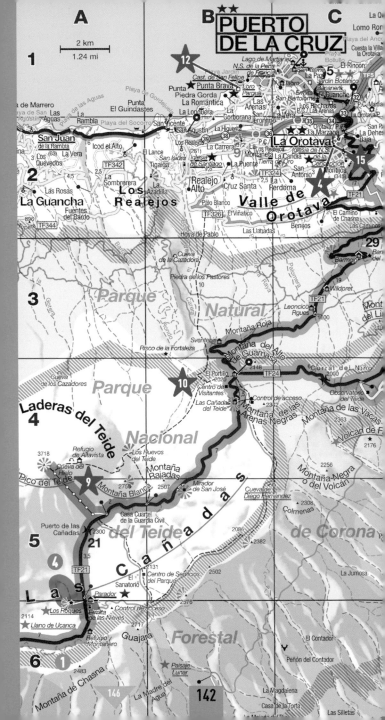

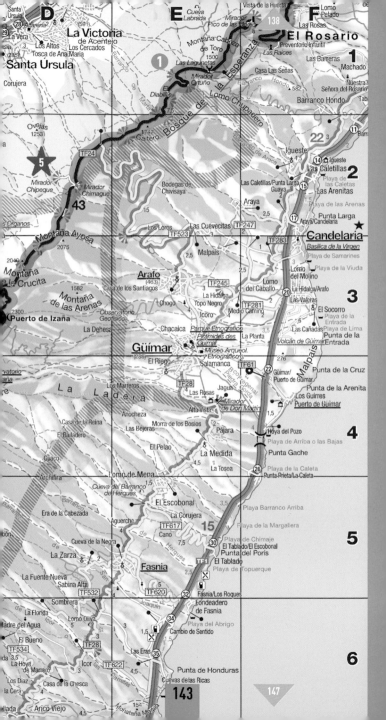

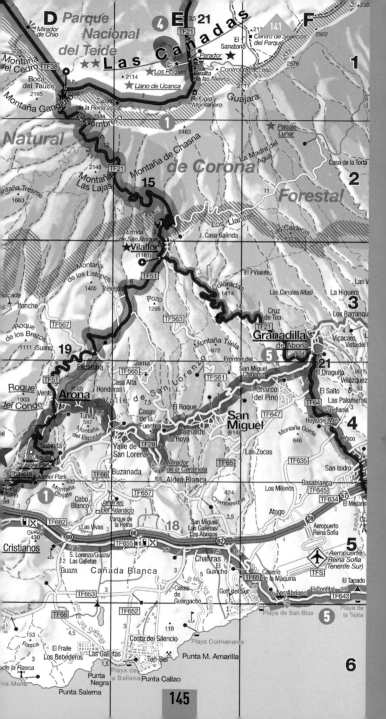

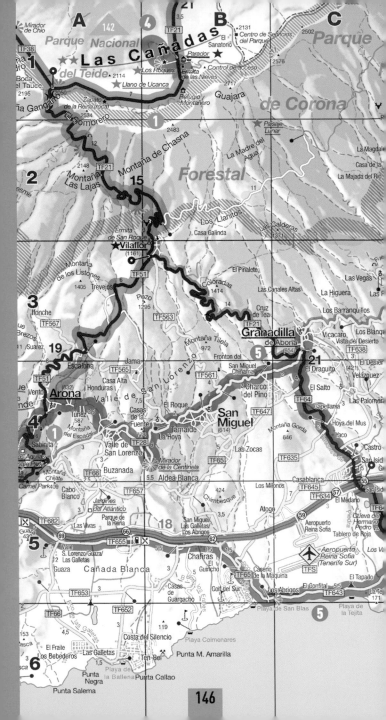

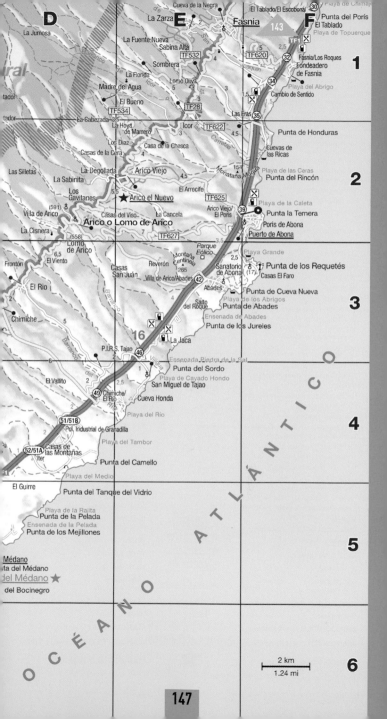

Cueva de la Negra
La Zarza
La Jumosa
Fasnia
El Tablado/El Escobonal
Punta del Porís
El Tablado
Playa de Topuerque
143
TF1
La Fuente Nueva
Sabina Alta
TF532
TF620
2,5
32
Fasnia/Los Roques
Fondeadero
de Fasnia
Sombrera
TF28
34
Madre del Agua
La Florida
Lomo Oliva
El Bueno
5
Playa del Abrigo
Cambio de Sentido
TF534
La Cabezada -3,5
Las Eras
5
35
Icor
TF622
4,5
Punta de Honduras
La Hoya
de Marrero
3
Casas de la Cera
Los Díaz
Casa de la Chesca
Cuevas de
las Ricas
La Degollada
La Sabinita
Arico Viejo
4,5
15¿
Montaña Médida
Playa de las Ceras
Punta del Rincón
Las Silletas
Los
Gavitanes
5,5
El Arrecife
TF625
Playa de la Caleta
Villa de Arico
(591)
Casas del Viso
La Cisnera
Arico o Lomo de Arico
La Cancela
7
(558)
TF627
Arico Viejo/
El Pons
39
Punta la Ternera
Poris de Abona
Puerto de Abona
Lomo
de Arico
3,5
Parque
Eólico
Playa Grande
Frontón
El Viento
Montaña
Centinela
265
Sanatorio
de Abona
(17)
Punta de los Requetés
Casas El Faro
El Río
2
Casas
San Juán
Reverón
Villa de Arico/Abades
42
Abades
Playa de los Abrigos
Punta de Cueva Nueva
Punta de Abades
Chimiche
5
Salto
del Roque
Ensenada de Abades
Punta de los Jureles
16
La Jaca
P.I.R.S. Tajao
46
Ensenada Piedra de la Sal
Punta del Sordo
Playa de Cayado Hondo
El Vallito
2,5
San Miguel de Tajao
Chimiche/
El Río
49
Cueva Honda
Playa del Río
51/518
Pol. Industrial de Granadilla
Playa del Tambor
52/51A
Casas de
las Montañas
iter
Punta del Camello
Playa del Medio
El Guirre
Punta del Tanque del Vidrio
Playa de la Rajita
Punta de la Pelada
Ensenada de la Pelada
Punta de los Mejillones
Médano
ta del Médano
del Médano
del Bocinegro

OCÉANO ATLÁNTICO

2 km
1.24 mi

1
2
3
4
5
6

147

KEY TO ROAD ATLAS

German	Symbol	English
Autobahn · Gebührenpflichtige Anschlussstelle · Gebührenstelle · Anschlussstelle mit Nummer · Rasthaus mit Übernachtung · Raststätte · Kleinraststätte · Tankstelle · Parkplatz mit und ohne WC	Trento	Motorway · Toll junction · Toll station · Junction with number · Motel · Restaurant · Snackbar · Filling-station · Parking place with and without WC
Autobahn in Bau und geplant mit Datum der voraussichtlichen Verkehrsübergabe	Datum / Date	Motorway under construction and projected with expected date of opening
Zweibahnige Straße (4-spurig)		Dual carriageway (4 lanes)
Fernverkehrsstraße · Straßennummern	14 · E45	Trunk road · Road numbers
Wichtige Hauptstraße		Important main road
Hauptstraße · Tunnel · Brücke		Main road · Tunnel · Bridge
Nebenstraßen		Minor roads
Fahrweg · Fußweg		Track · Footpath
Wanderweg (Auswahl)		Tourist footpath (selection)
Eisenbahn mit Fernverkehr		Main line railway
Zahnradbahn, Standseilbahn		Rack-railway, funicular
Kabinenschwebebahn · Sessellift		Aerial cableway · Chair-lift
Autofähre · Personenfähre		Car ferry · Passenger ferry
Schifffahrtslinie		Shipping route
Naturschutzgebiet · Sperrgebiet		Nature reserve · Prohibited area
Nationalpark · Naturpark · Wald		National park · natural park · Forest
Straße für Kfz. gesperrt	X X X X X	Road closed to motor vehicles
Straße mit Gebühr		Toll road
Straße mit Wintersperre	XII-II	Road closed in winter
Straße für Wohnanhänger gesperrt bzw. nicht empfehlenswert		Road closed or not recommended for caravans
Touristenstraße · Pass	Weinstraße · 1510	Tourist route · Pass
Schöner Ausblick · Rundblick · Landschaftlich bes. schöne Strecke		Scenic view · Panoramic view · Route with beautiful scenery
Heilbad · Schwimmbad		Spa · Swimming pool
Jugendherberge · Campingplatz		Youth hostel · Camping site
Golfplatz · Sprungschanze		Golf-course · Ski jump
Kirche im Ort, freistehend · Kapelle		Church · Chapel
Kloster · Klosterruine		Monastery · Monastery ruin
Synagoge · Moschee		Synagogue · Mosque
Schloss, Burg · Schloss-, Burgruine		Palace, castle · Ruin
Turm · Funk-, Fernsehturm		Tower · Radio-, TV-tower
Leuchtturm · Kraftwerk		Lighthouse · Power station
Wasserfall · Schleuse		Waterfall · Lock
Bauwerk · Marktplatz, Areal		Important building · Market place, area
Ausgrabungs- u. Ruinenstätte · Bergwerk		Arch. excavation, ruins · Mine
Dolmen · Menhir · Nuraghen		Dolmen · Menhir · Nuraghe
Hünen-, Hügelgrab · Soldatenfriedhof		Cairn · Military cemetery
Hotel, Gasthaus, Berghütte · Höhle		Hotel, inn, refuge · Cave

Kultur		**Culture**
Malerisches Ortsbild · Ortshöhe	WIEN (171)	Picturesque town · Elevation
Eine Reise wert	★★ MILANO	Worth a journey
Lohnt einen Umweg	★ TEMPLIN	Worth a detour
Sehenswert	Andermatt	Worth seeing

Landschaft		**Landscape**
Eine Reise wert	★★ Las Cañadas	Worth a journey
Lohnt einen Umweg	★ Texel	Worth a detour
Sehenswert	Dikti	Worth seeing

MARCO POLO Erlebnistour 1		**MARCO POLO Discovery Tour 1**
MARCO POLO Erlebnistouren		**MARCO POLO Discovery Tours**
MARCO POLO Highlight	★	**MARCO POLO Highlight**

FOR YOUR NEXT TRIP...

MARCO POLO TRAVEL GUIDES

Travel with
**Insider
Tips**

INDEX

This index lists all sights, museums and destinations plus the main squares and streets, the key terms and people featured in this guide. Numbers in bold indicate a main entry.

WRITE TO US

e-mail: sales@heartwoodpublishing.co.uk

Did you have a great holiday? Is there something on your mind? Whatever it is, let us know! Whether you want to praise, alert us to errors or give us a personal tip – MARCO POLO would be pleased to hear from you.

We do everything we can to provide the very latest information for your trip. Nevertheless, despite all of our authors' thorough research, errors can creep in. MARCO POLO does not accept any liability for this. Please contact us by e-mail.

PICTURE CREDITS
Cover photograph: Parque Rural de Anaga (Schapowalow/SIME: P. Arcangelo)
Photos: O. Baumli (120/121); DuMont Bildarchiv: Schwarzbach/Schröder (30/31, 37, 120); © fotolia.com: Rohit Seth (18 bottom); R. Freyer (4 bottom, 14, 20/21, 28 left, 32/33, 40/41, 46/47, 54, 58/59, 67, 84); I. Gawin (74); R. Hackenberg (flap right, 57); huber-images: O. Fantuz (87, 105), H.-P. Huber (71, 82), Mirau (68/69), A. Piai (96/97), R. Schmid (12/13), R. Schmid (26/27, 34, 49, 61, 108, 118), F. Vallenari (52/53); ITER - Instituto Tecnológico y de Energías Renovables, S. A. (18 top); Laif: M. Gumm (62), G. Knechtel (46), Sasse (77, 122 top), M. Sasse (91), Tophoven (19 top); Laif/hemis: R. Soberka (10); Laif/hemis.fr: Frilet (92/93); Look/age fotostock (115, 122 bottom); Lookphotos: J. Richter (19 bottom); mauritius images: K. Neuner (2, 88); mauritius images/age (28 right, 39), mauritius images/Alamy (4 o., 5, 7, 8, 9, 11, 16/17, 24, 43, 45, 51, 78/79, 94, 102, 111, 116/117, 123); mauritius images/Author's Images (80); mauritius images/CuboImages (64/65); mauritius images/imagebroker: Kreder (72/73), Sarti (6); mauritius images/John Warburton-Lee: G. Hellier (18 M.); mauritius images/Rubberball (3); D. Renckhoff (30, 112/113, 121); Schapowalow/SIME: P. Arcangelo (1 top); White Star: M. Gumm (flap left, 29, 31, 134/135); E. Wrba (22)

3nd Edition – fully revised and updated 2018
Worldwide Distribution: Heartwood Publishing Ltd, Bath, United Kingdom. Email: sales@heartwoodpublishing.co.uk
© MAIRDUMONT GmbH & Co. KG, Ostfildern
Chief editor: Marion Zorn; Author: Sven Weniger, Co-author: Izabella Gawin; Editor: Arnd M. Schuppius
Programme supervision: Tamara Hub, Ann-Katrin Kutzner, Nikolai Michaelis, Kristin Schimpf, Martin Silbermann
Picture editor: Gabriele Forst, Stefanie Wiese; What's hot: Izabella Gawin; wunder media, München Cartography road atlas/pull-out map: © MAIRDUMONT, Ostfildern
Design: milchhof:atelier, Berlin; design cover, p. 1, cover pull-out map: Karl Anders – Büro für Visual Stories, Hamburg; design p. 2/3, Discovery Tours: Susan Chaaban Dipl.-Des. (FH)
Translated from German by Paul Fletcher, Suffolk; Susan Jones, Tübingen; Beste Worte GmbH, Berlin; editor of the English edition: Tony Halliday, Oxford; Neue Werte GmbH, Berlin
Prepress: Beste Worte GmbH, Berlin
Phrase book in cooperation with Ernst Klett Sprachen GmbH, Stuttgart, Editorial by Pons Wörterbücher

MIX
Paper from
responsible sources
FSC® C016779

DOS & DON'TS

A few things to bear in mind on Tenerife

GOING INTO THE WATER WHEN THERE'S A RED FLAG

More than 70 people have drowned on the coasts of the Canary Islands since 2016. Often due to carelessness. Many people underestimate the strength of the surf and the current and overestimate their own strength. If the red flag is raised at the beach, you should stay out of the water. Yellow indicates that you should be cautious, and if the flag is green, you can jump right in – although you should never swim out too far.

DON'T LEAVE VALUABLES IN YOUR CAR

Hire cars are often broken into, and bags and wallets stolen from the beach or hotel room. So don't leave anything of value in your car or in the boot. Similarly make sure anything of value is locked away in your room or apartment safe. If no safe is available, then leave any valuables at reception.

TAKING PLANTS

Calla lilies, cactus-like euphorbia, mini dragon trees – some visitors can't help but dig up these indigenous plants to give them a new home on their balcony. But be careful. Canarian plants are subject to special protection and they cannot be removed from the islands. Instead, buy a bag of seeds in a flower shop (*jardinería*) – you can transport them easier too.

GETTING SCAMMED

Bread is part of every meal in Spain. It used to be free. Now they will serve it without a word even if you didn't order it... and charge you for it after your meal. If you are legitimately dissatisfied, ask for an *hoja de reclamación* (complaint form) to write down your criticism (in English). All Spanish service providers, i.e. taxis, accommodation, supermarkets etc. must make them available visibly. These business are strictly monitored by the state and their licences can be revoked if multiple complaints are filed against them.

GOING INTO THE MOUNTAINS SCANTILY CLAD

Wearing flip-flops in the national park? No way! Holidaymakers often wear summery clothes on the sunny coast, only to be surprised by the icy temperatures later on. This is a perfect way to get a cold... The rule of thumb is: for every 100 m (330 ft) in elevation, the temperature drops by 1°C. So if it's 23°C when you leave the coast and you drive up to over 2,000m (6,600 ft), it's possible that it will be 3°C when you get out of the car. So do take a warm coat and closed footwear.

DON'T USE THE HOTEL INTERNET NETWORK

Many hotels make internet access available for guests. But the charges can often be very high. Internet access should be free these days.